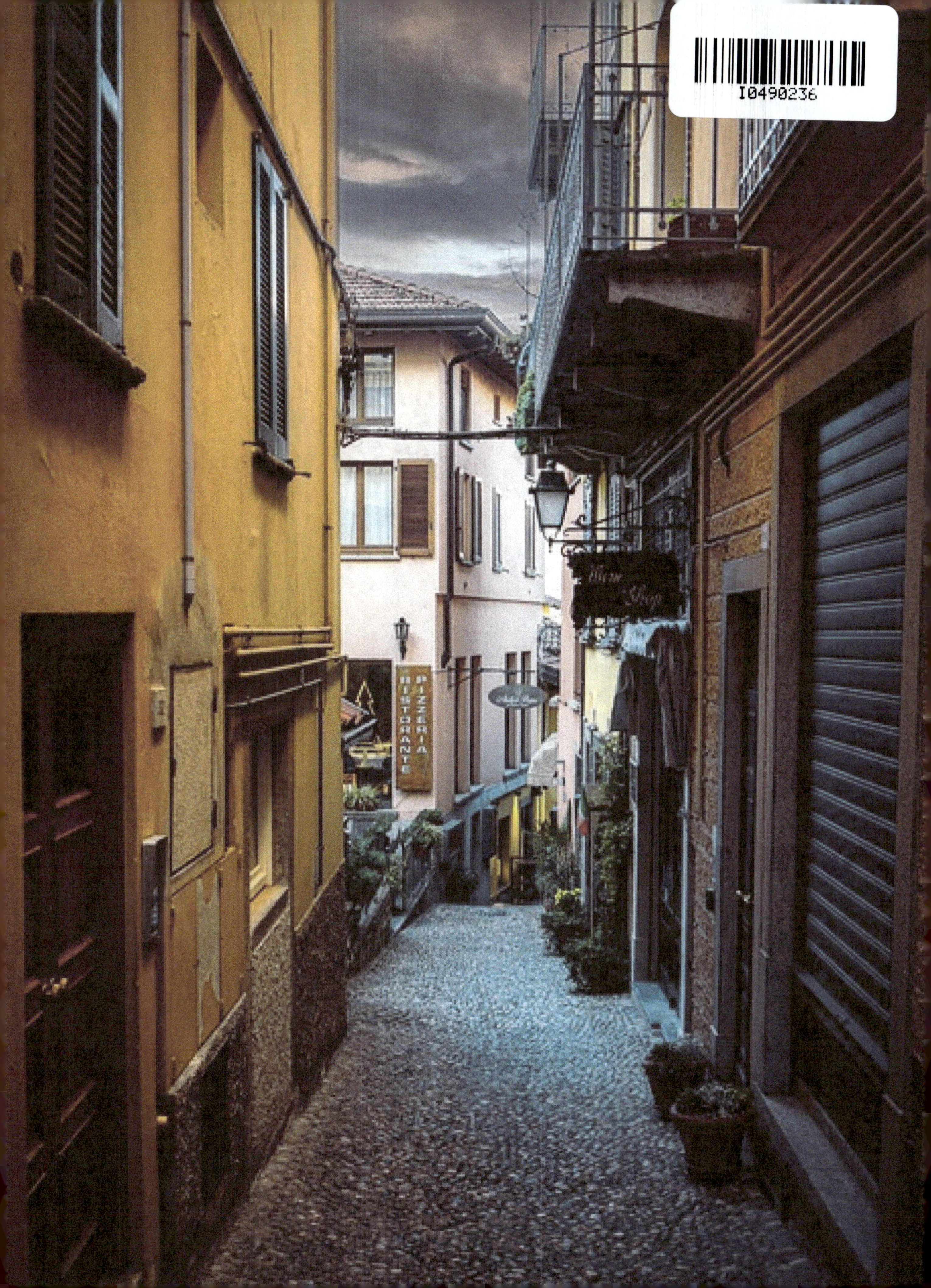
RISTORANTE
PIZZERIA

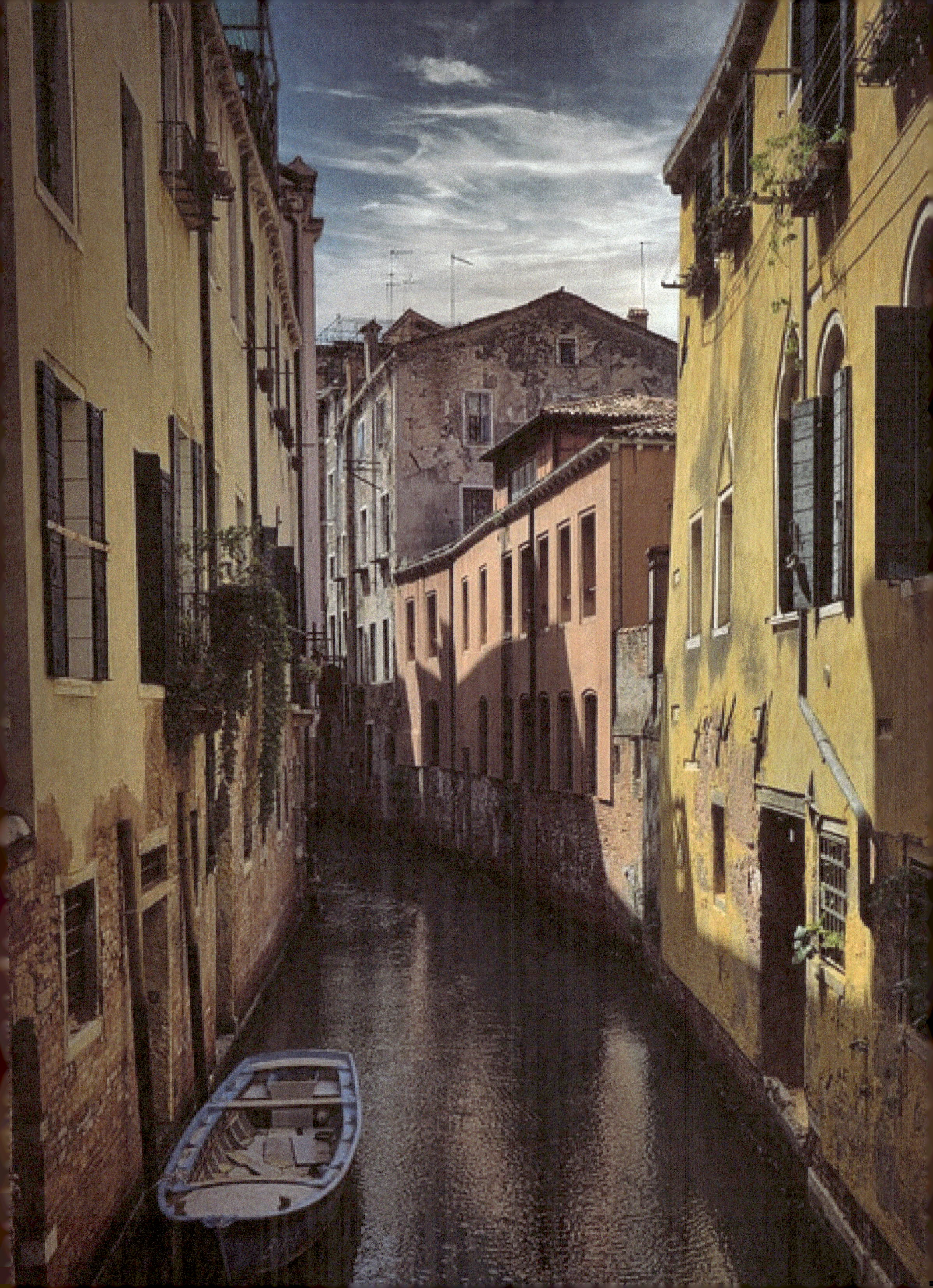

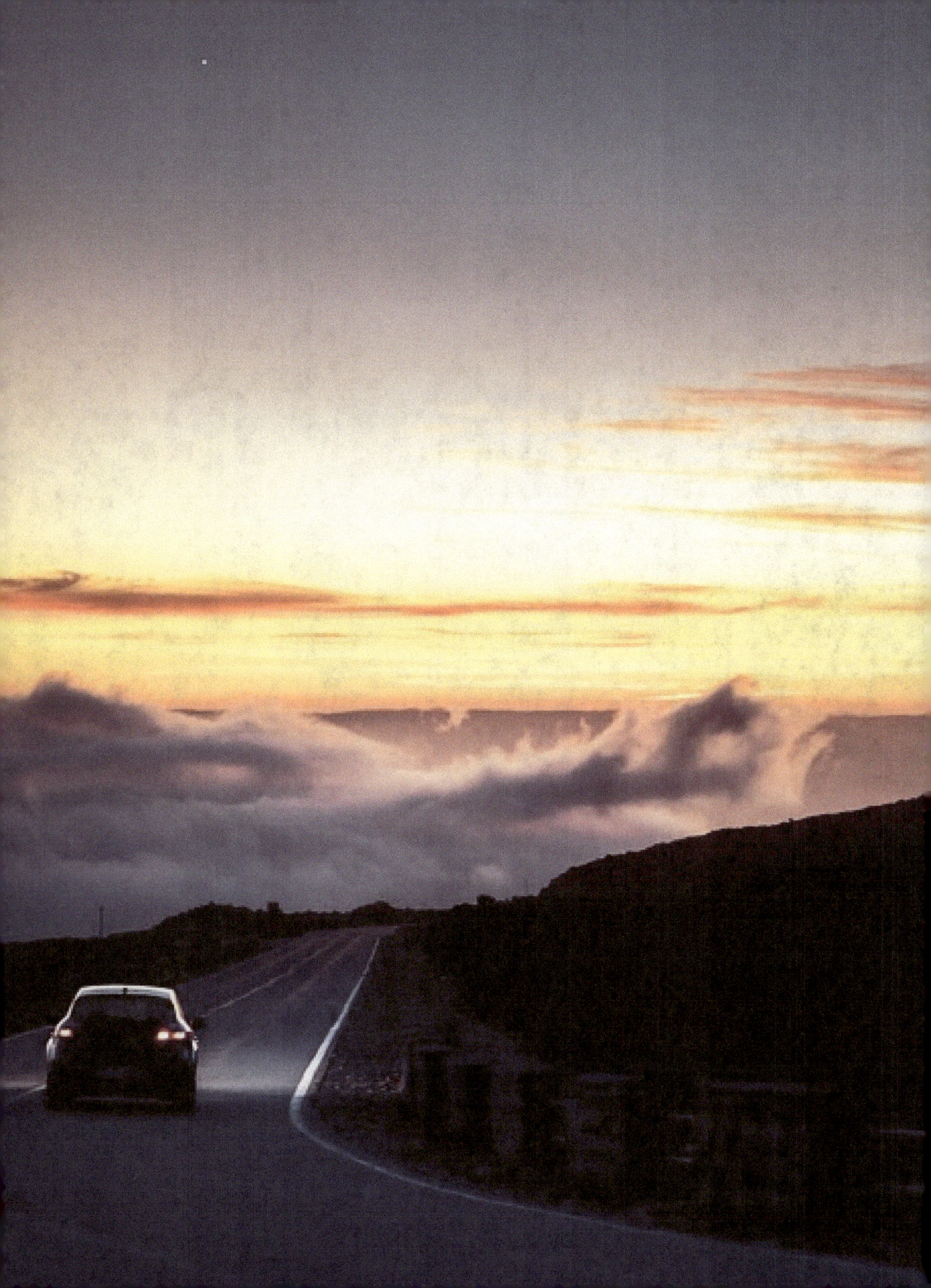

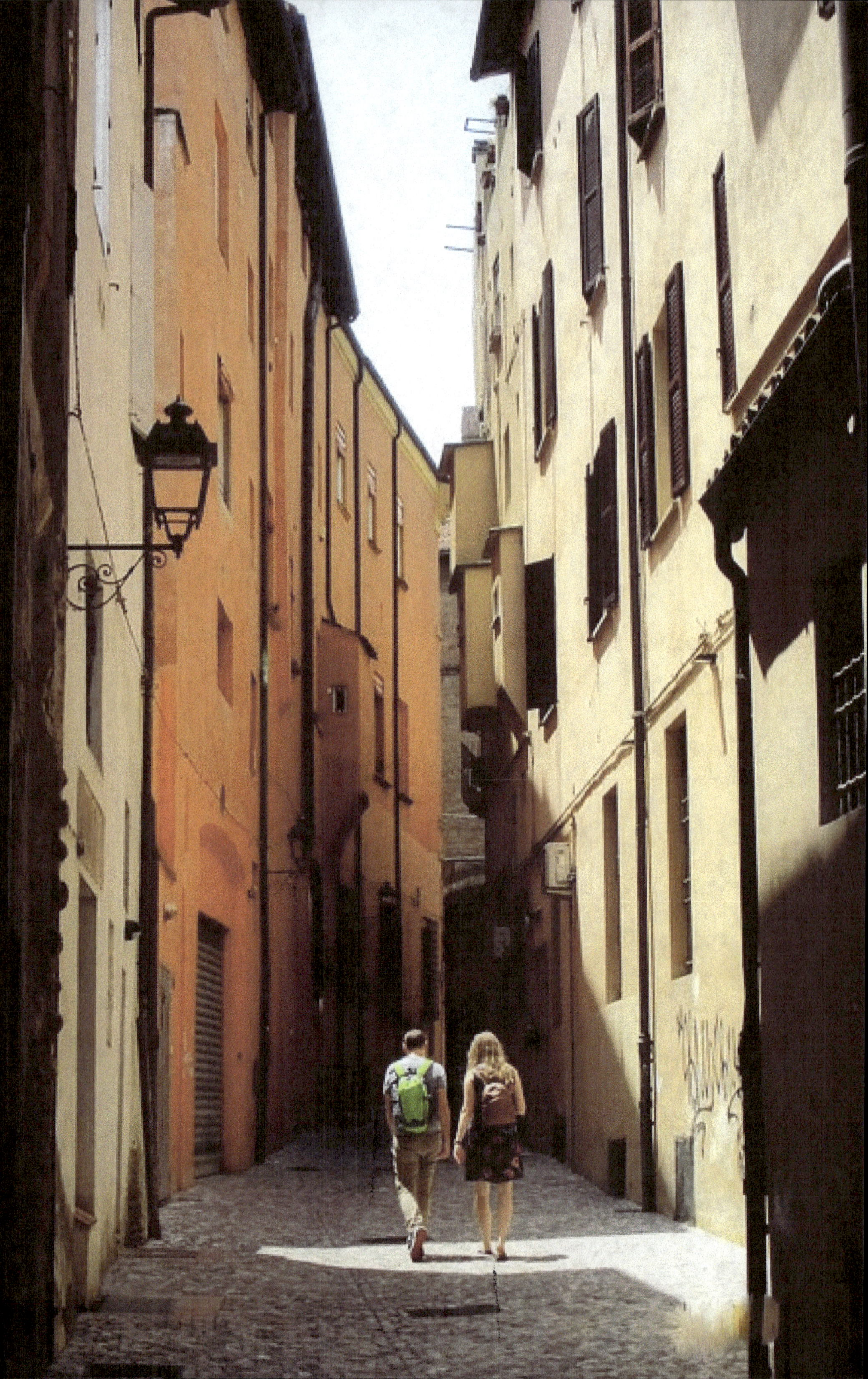

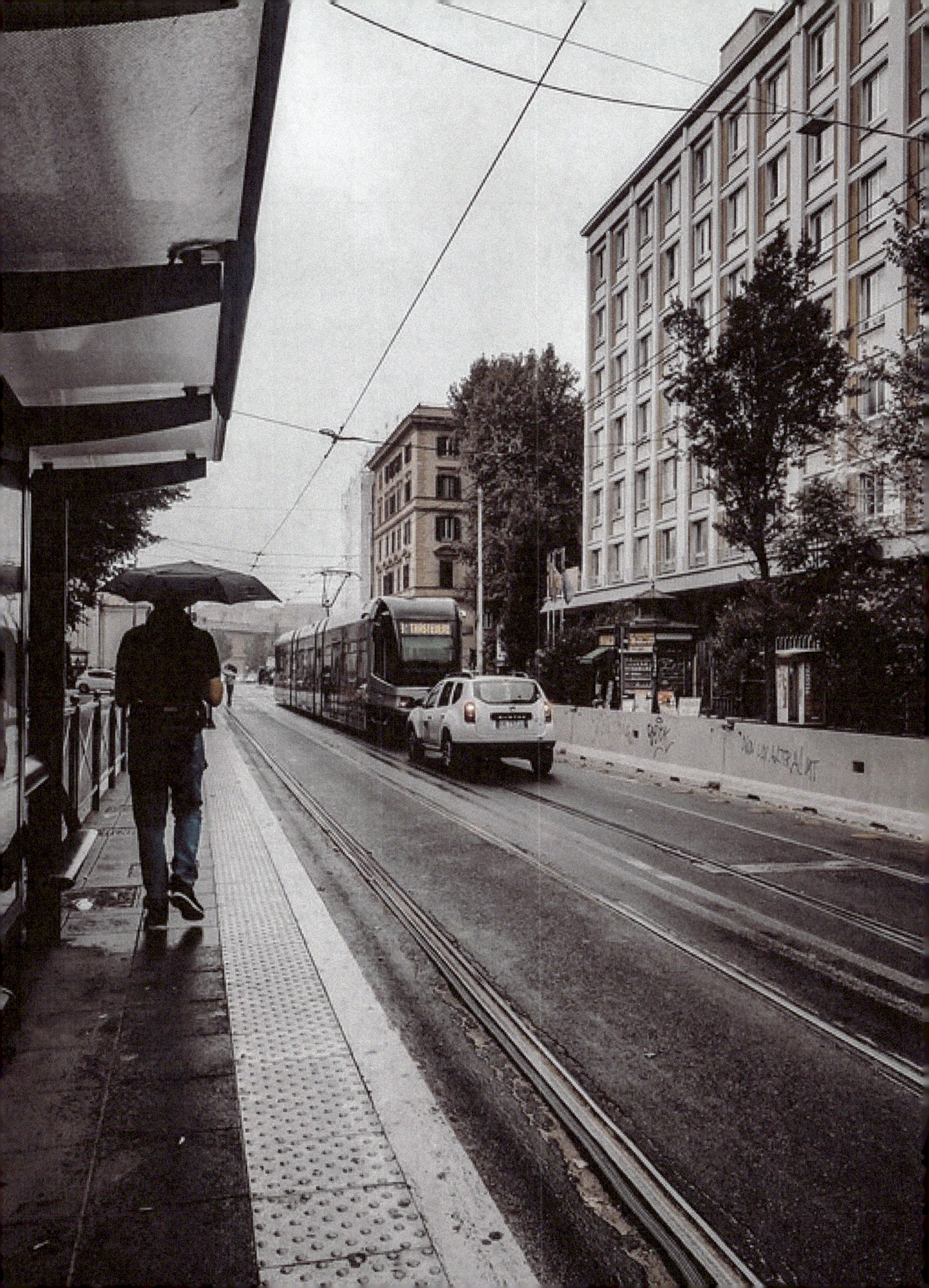

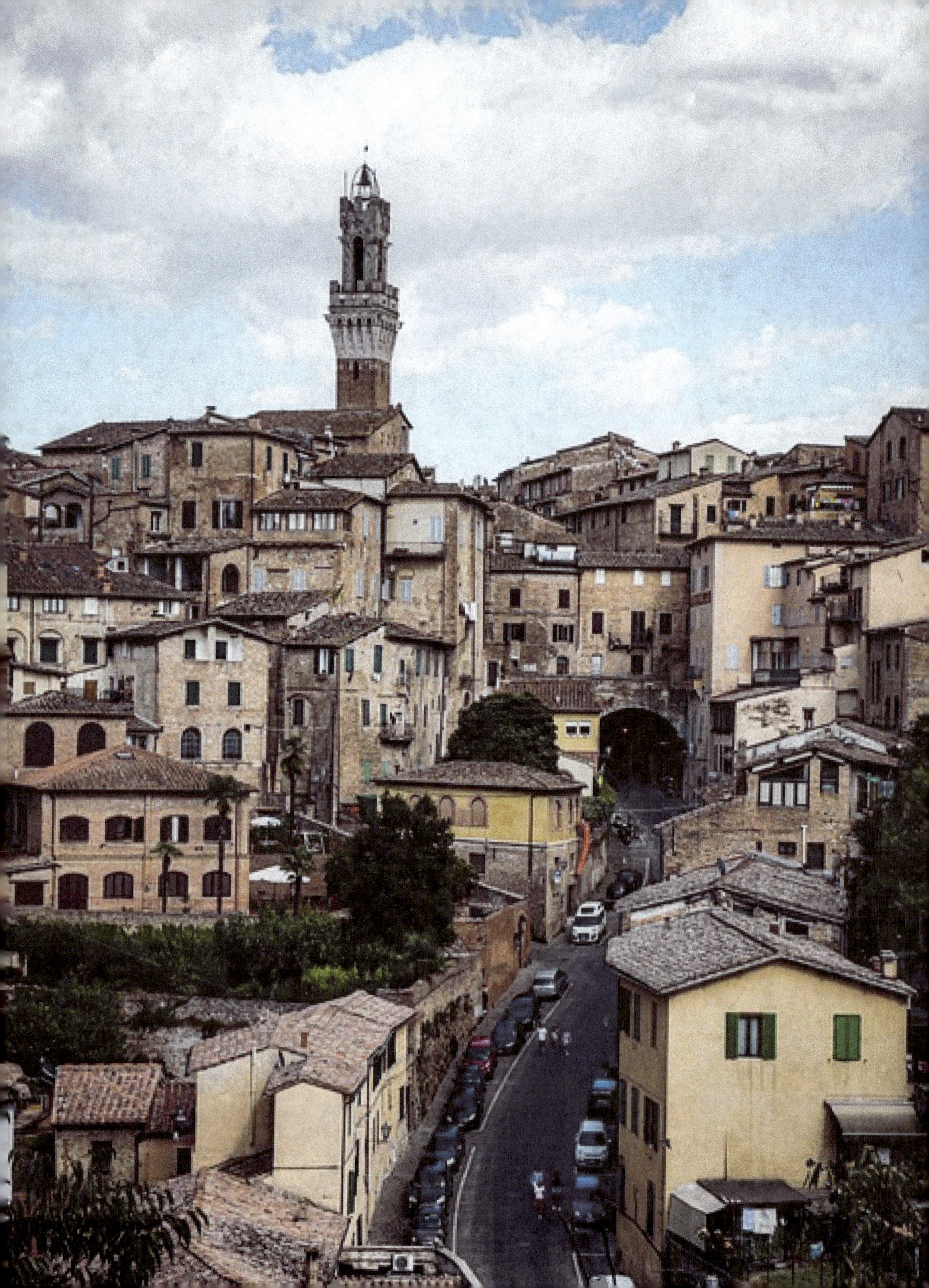

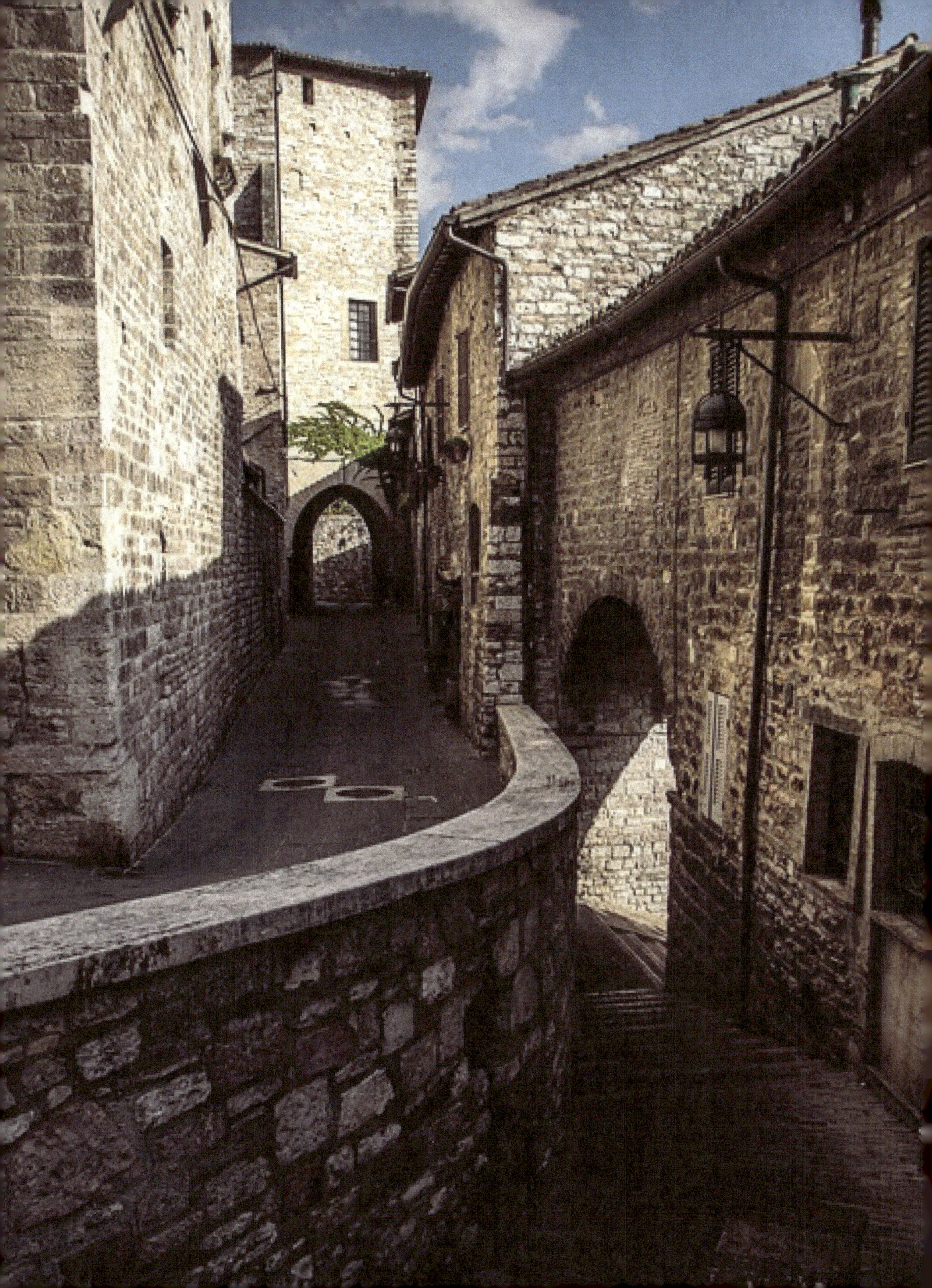

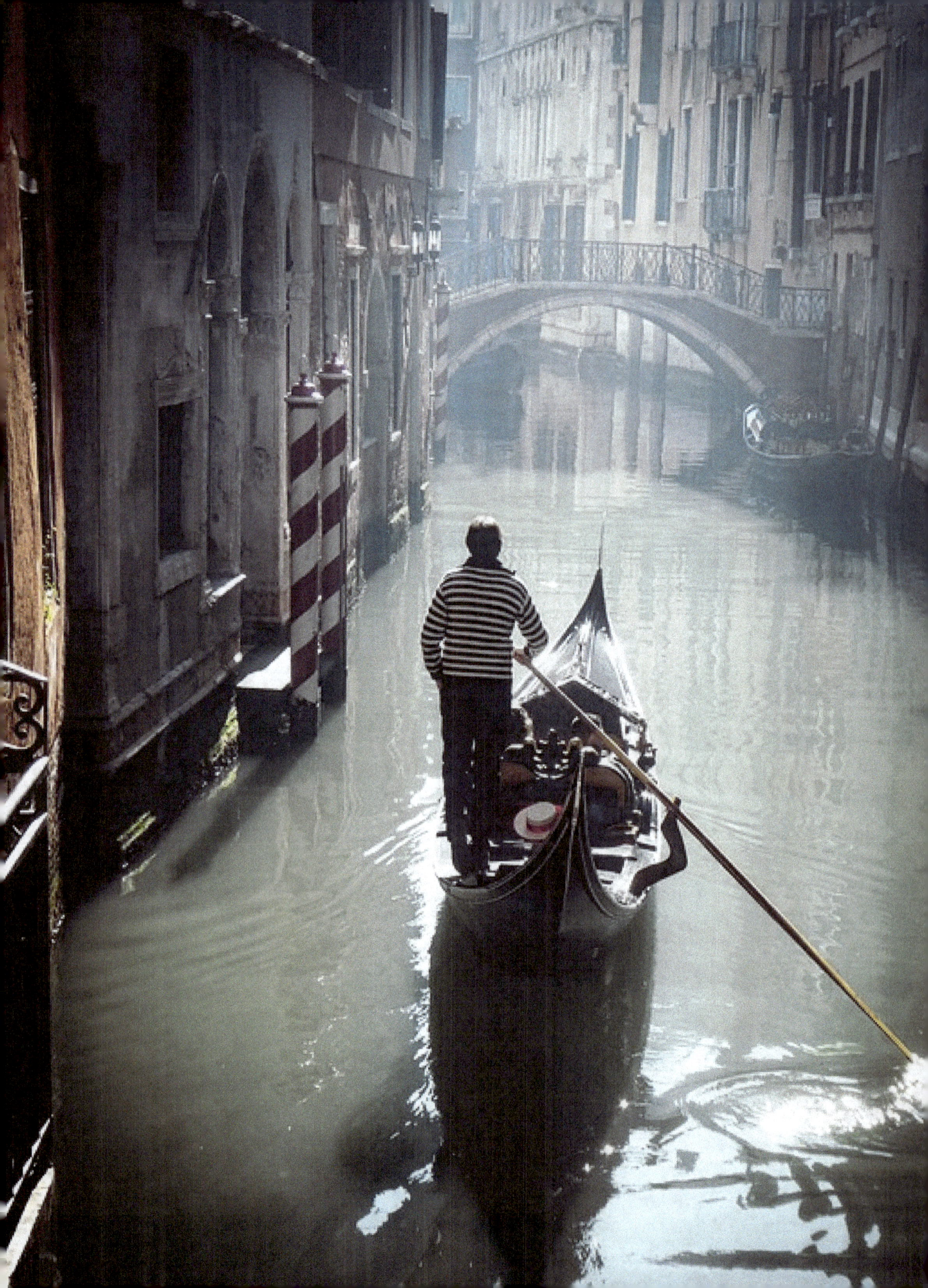

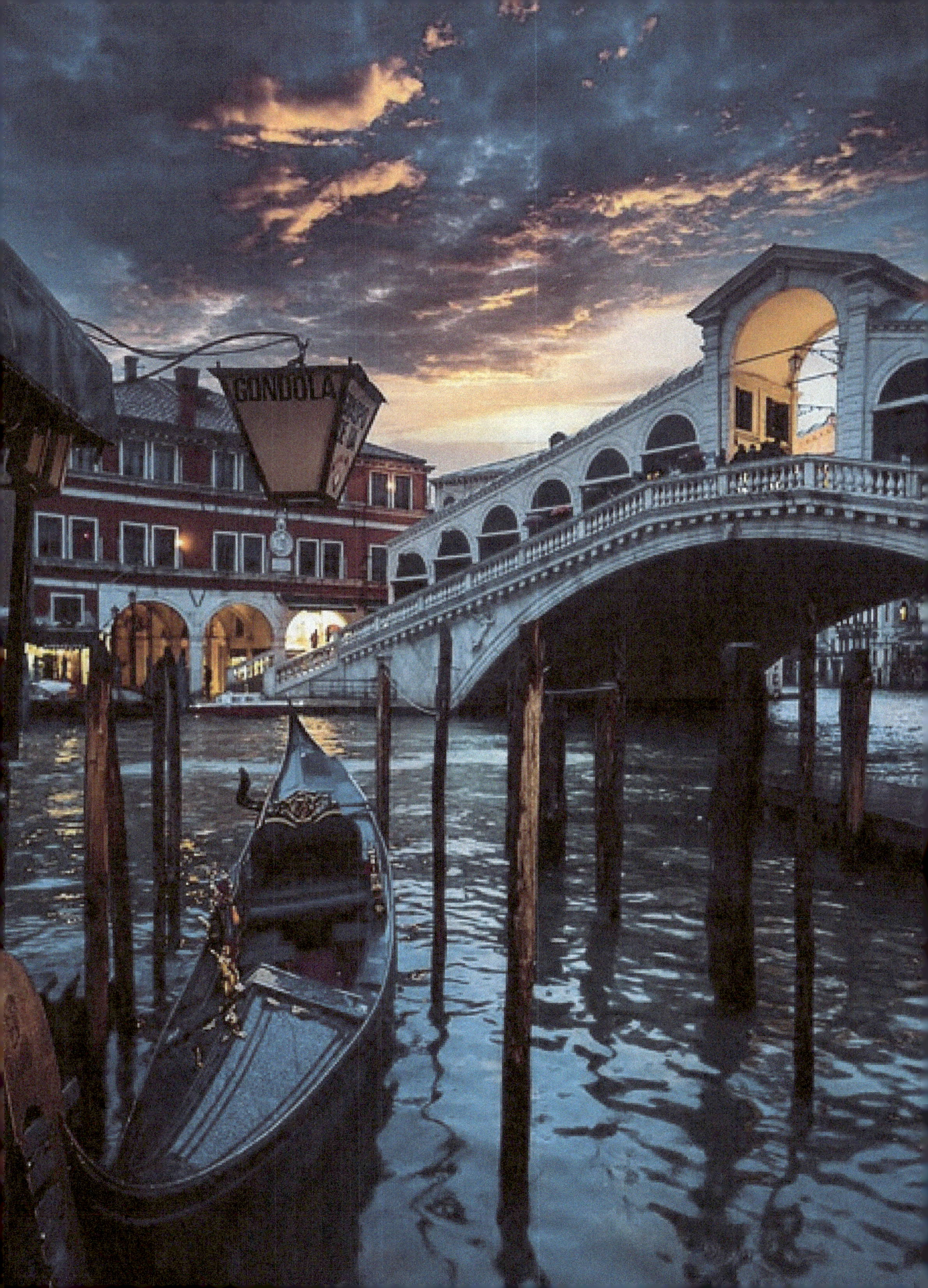
GONDOLA

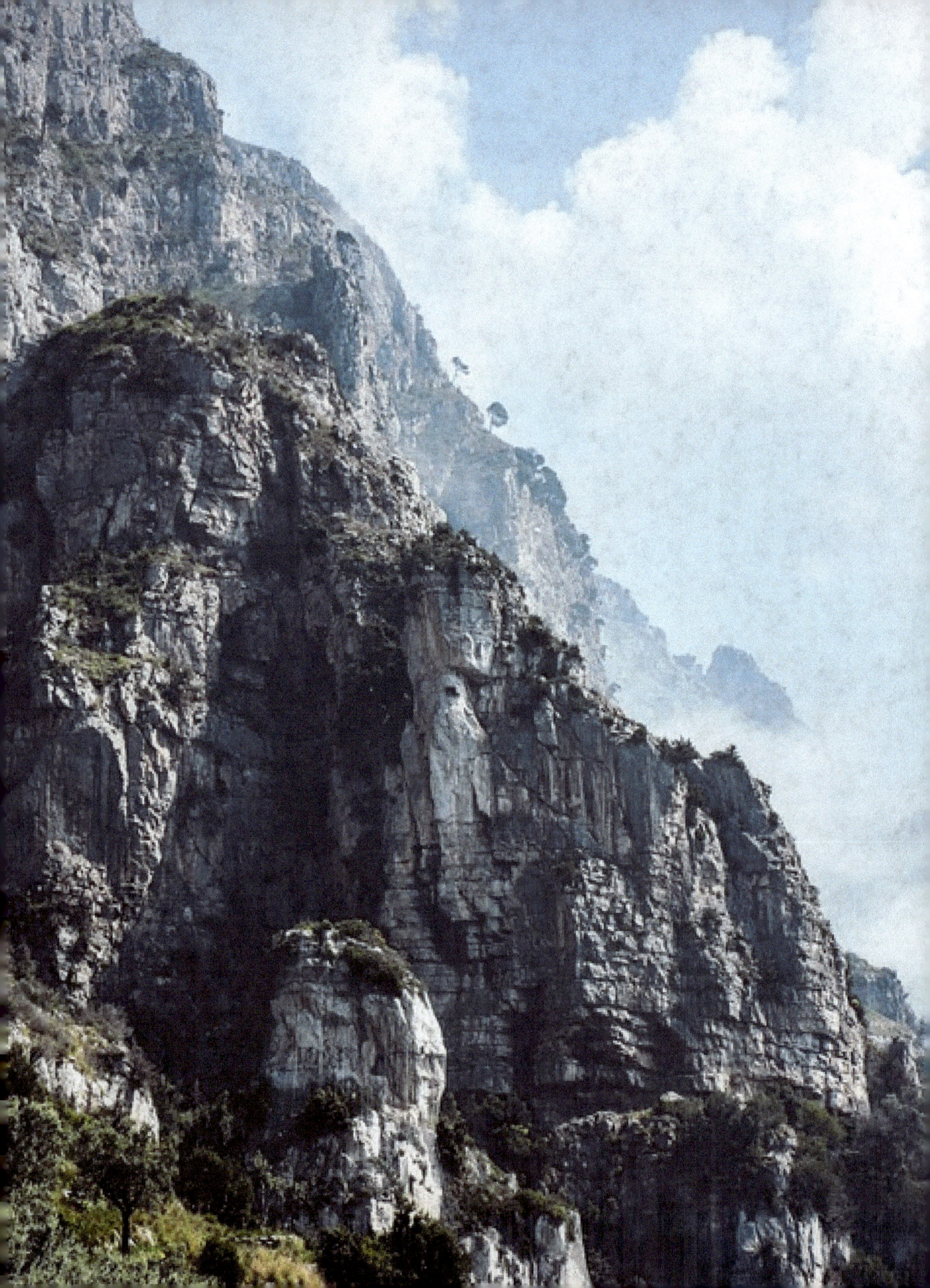

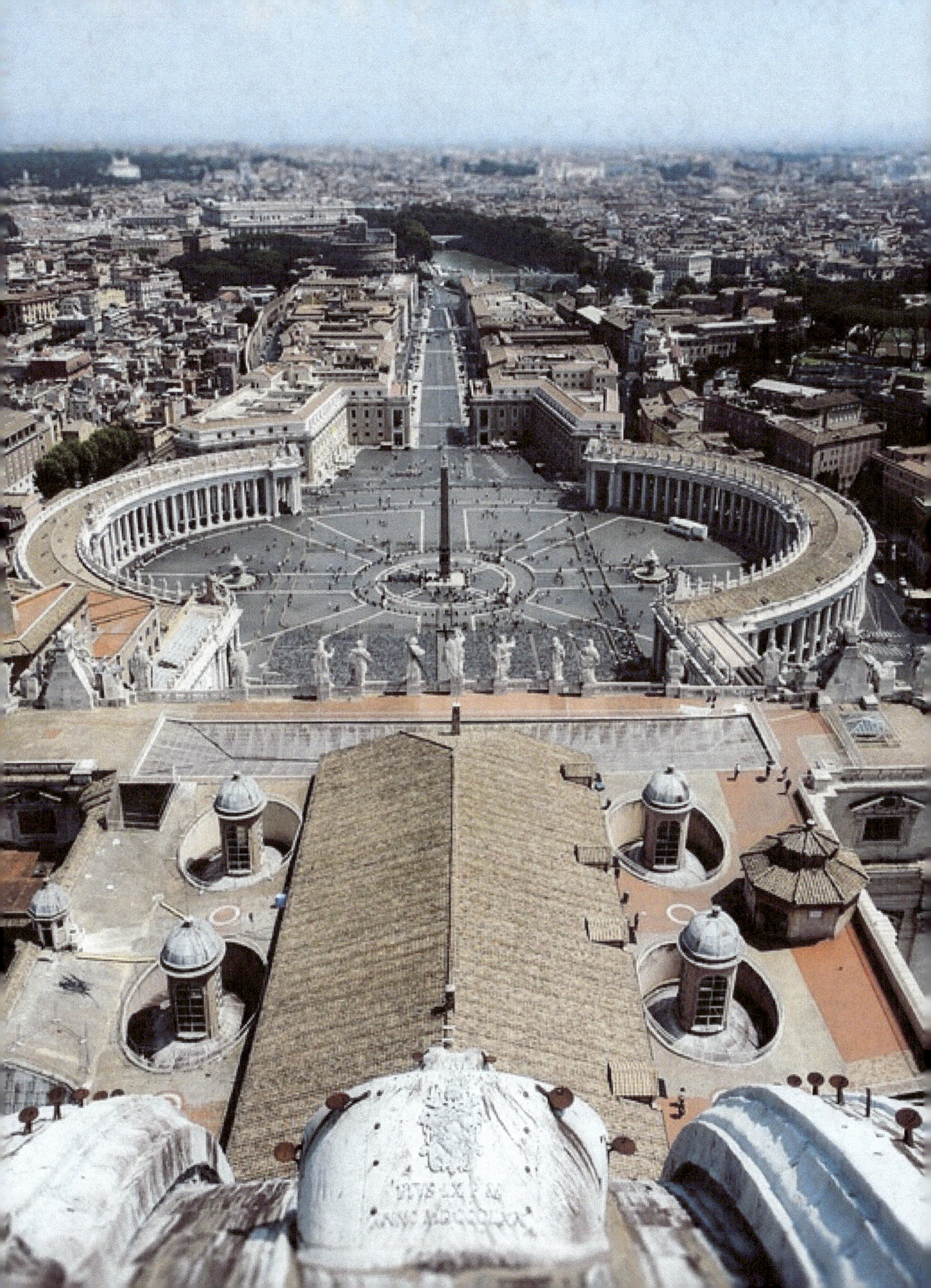

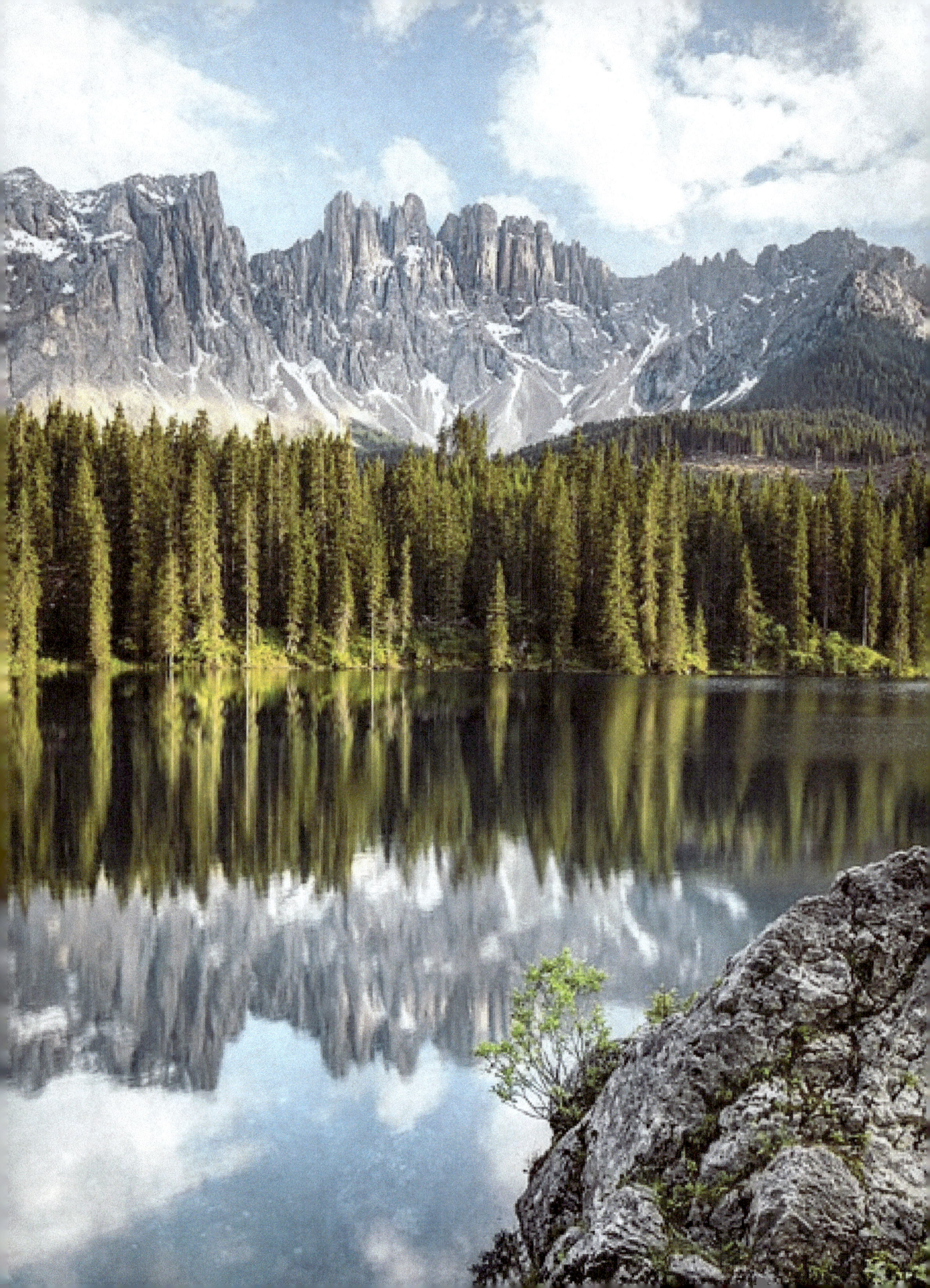

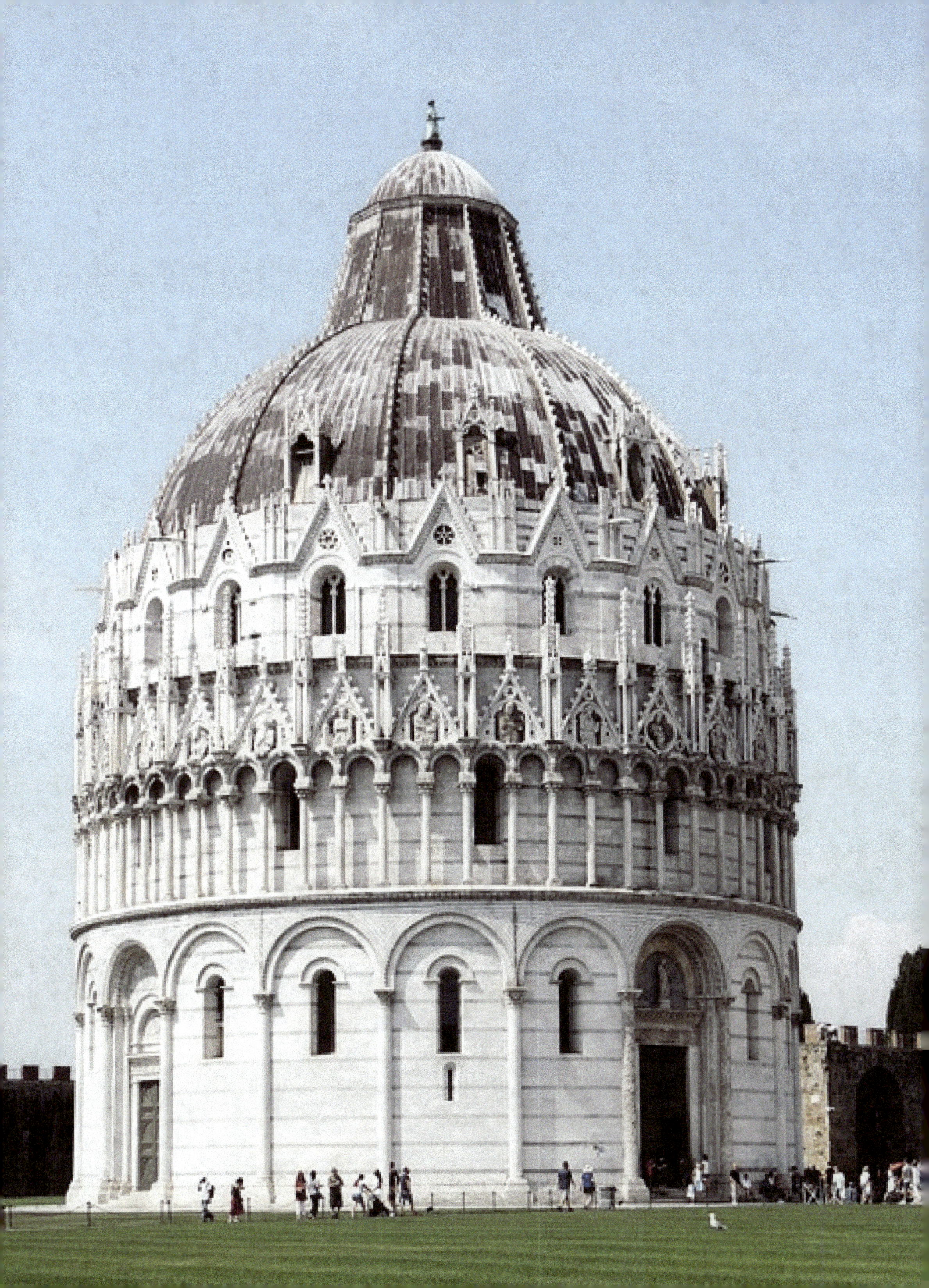

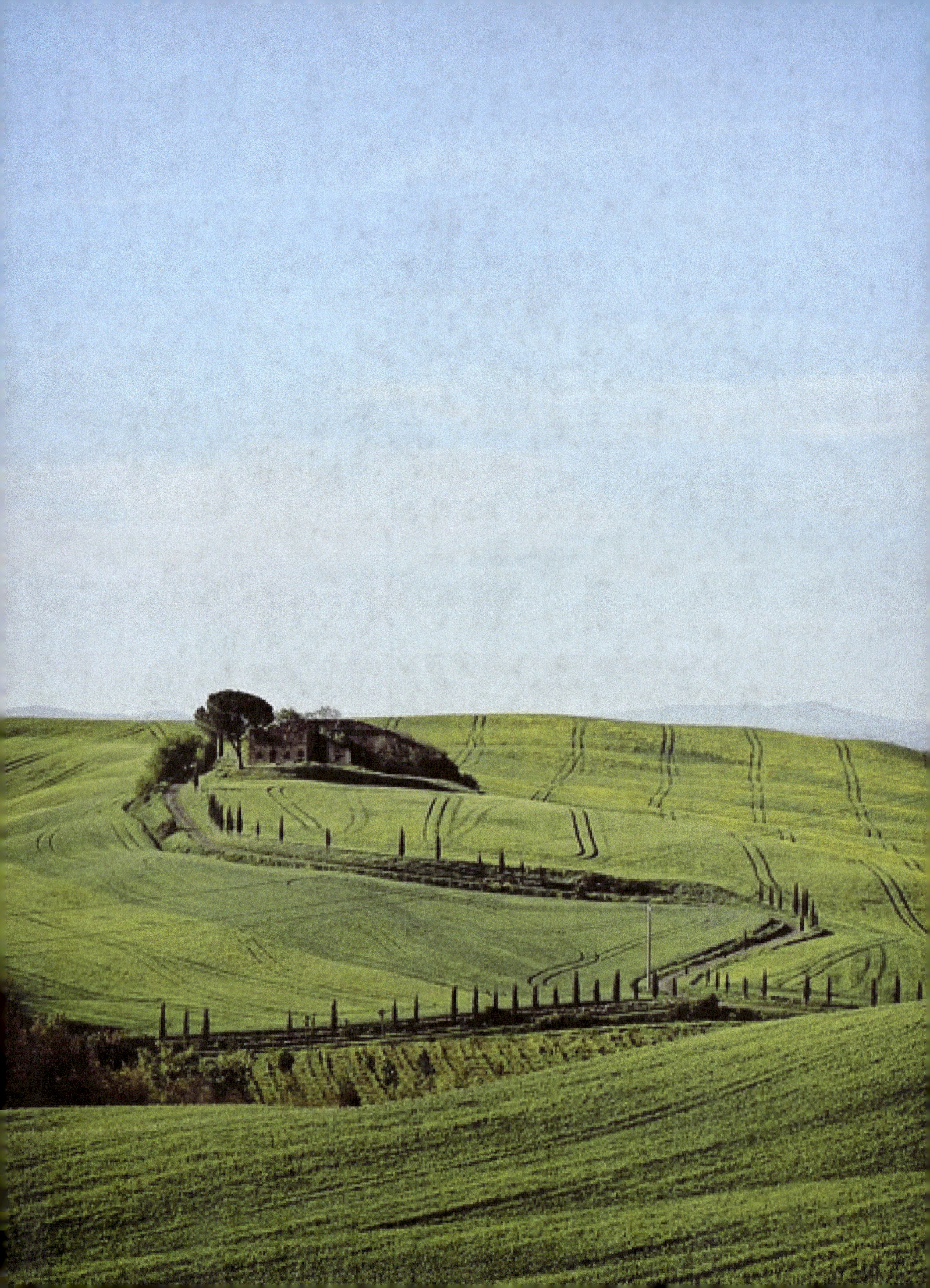

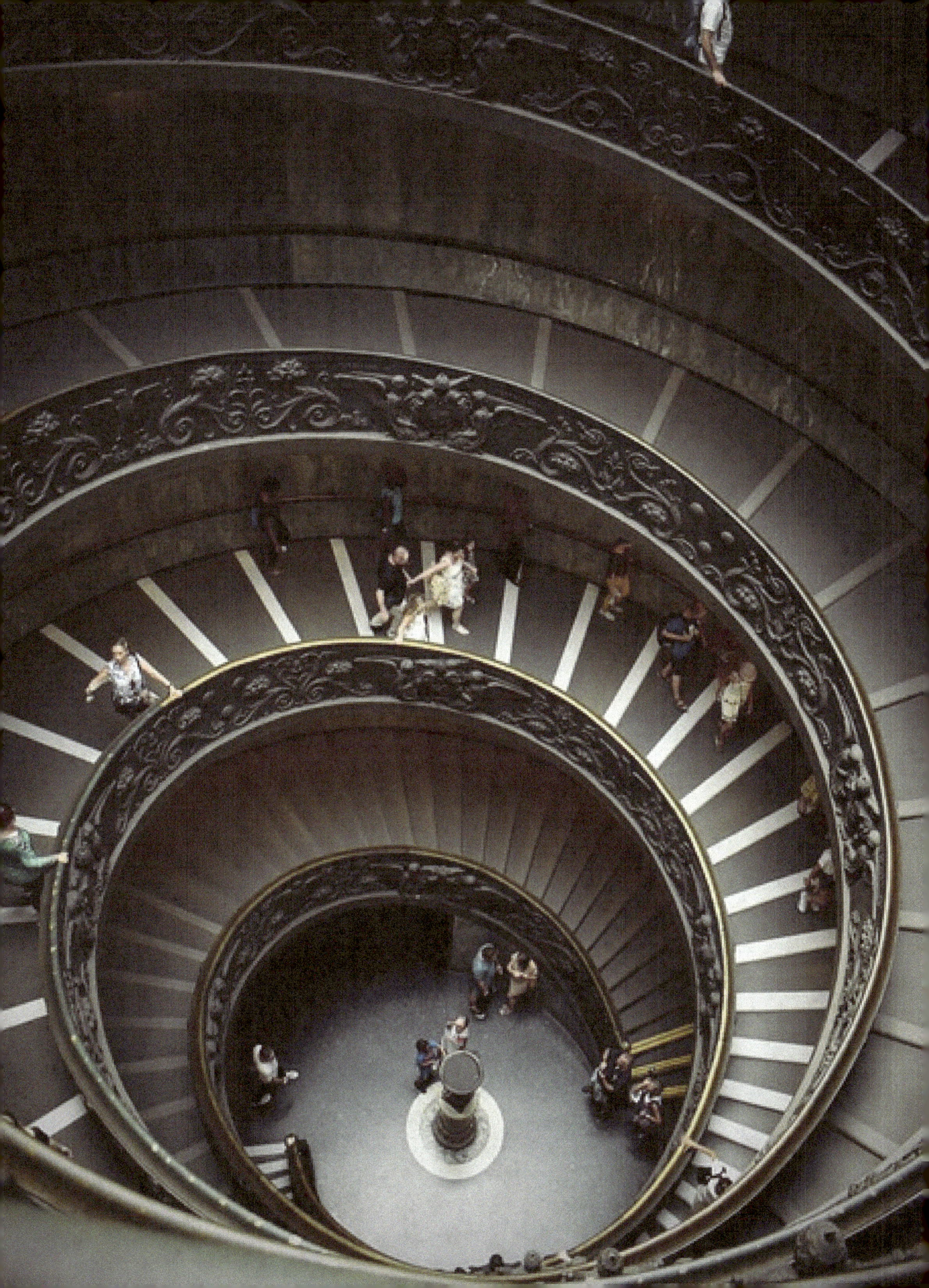

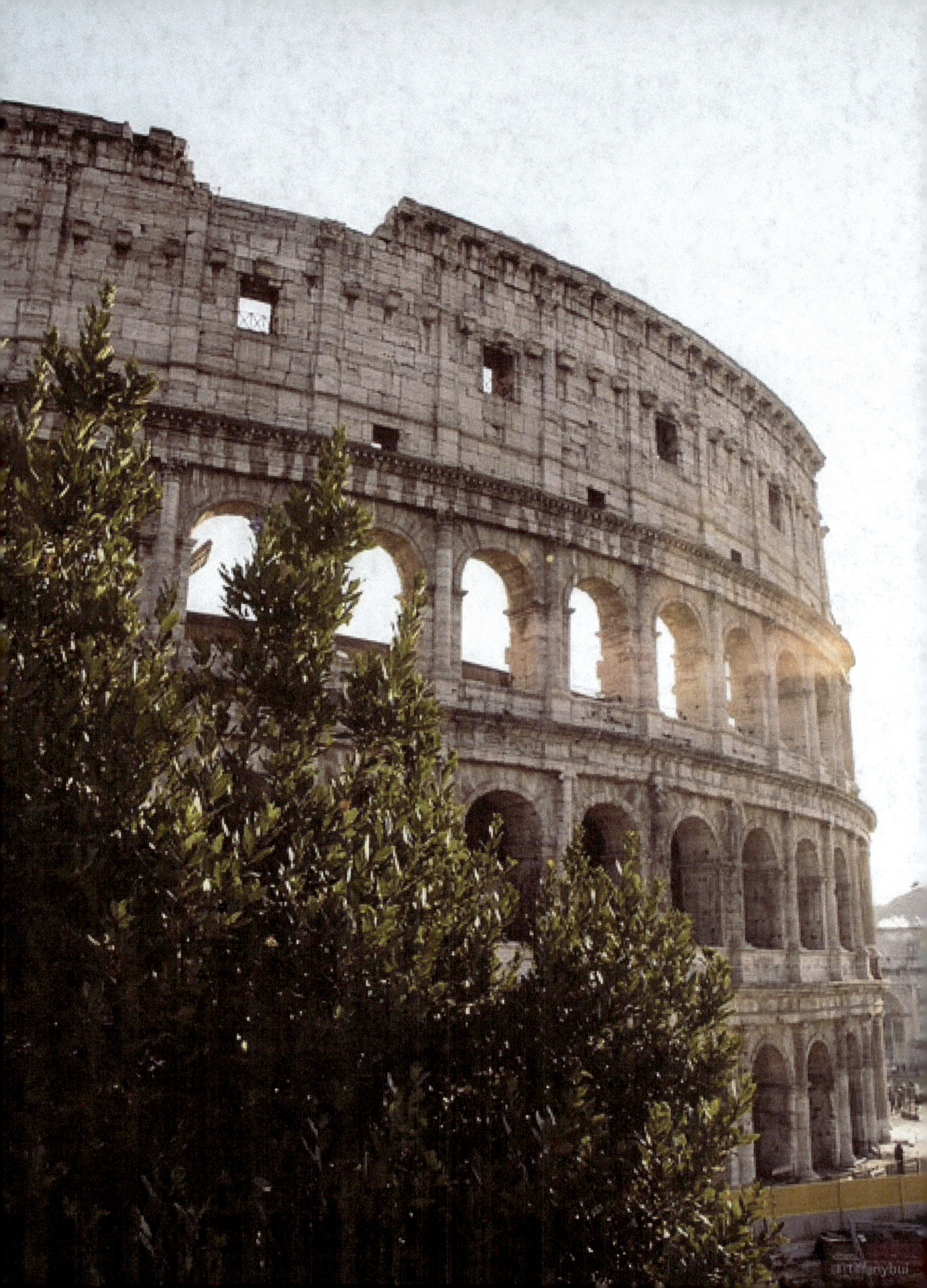

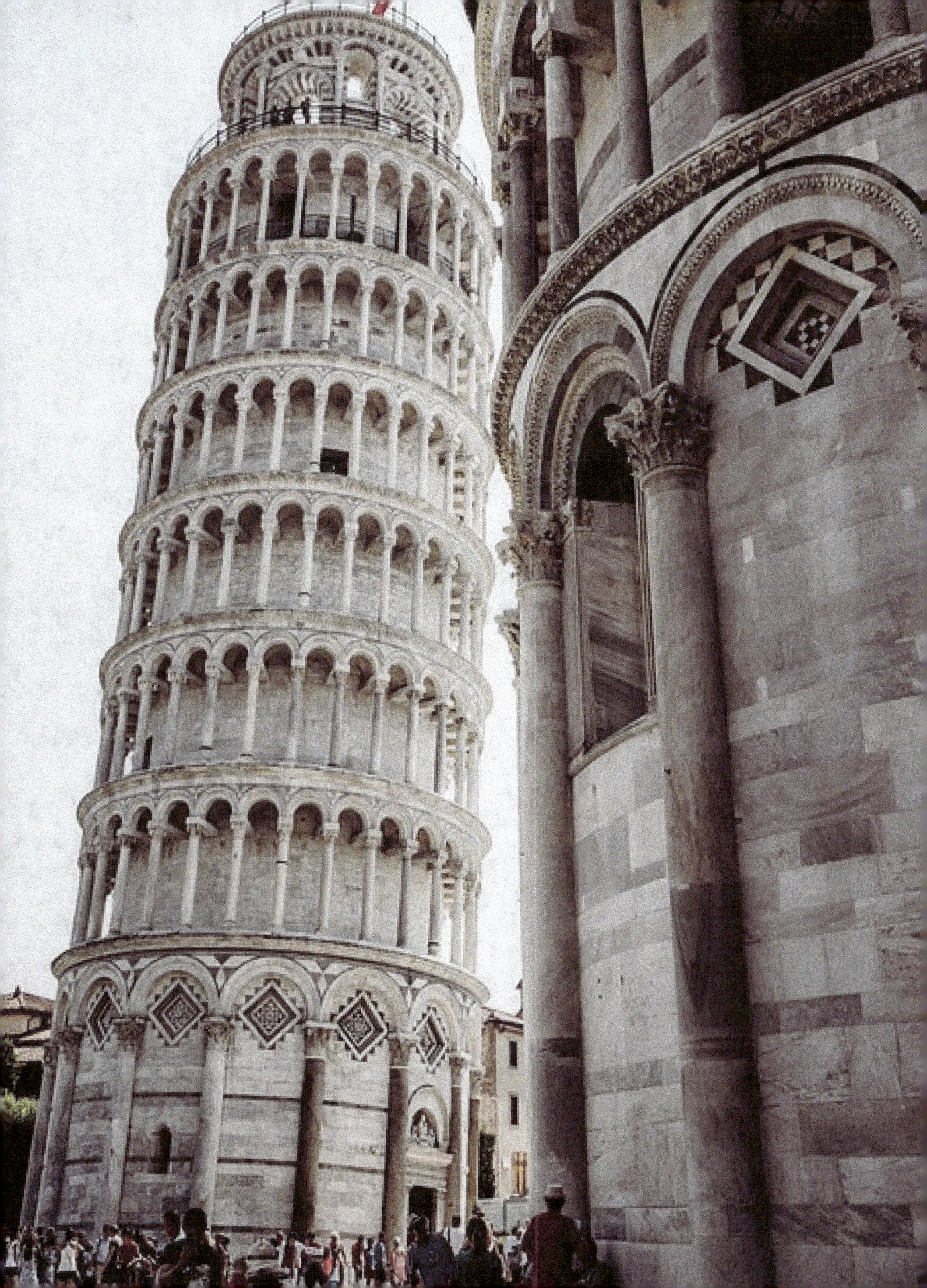

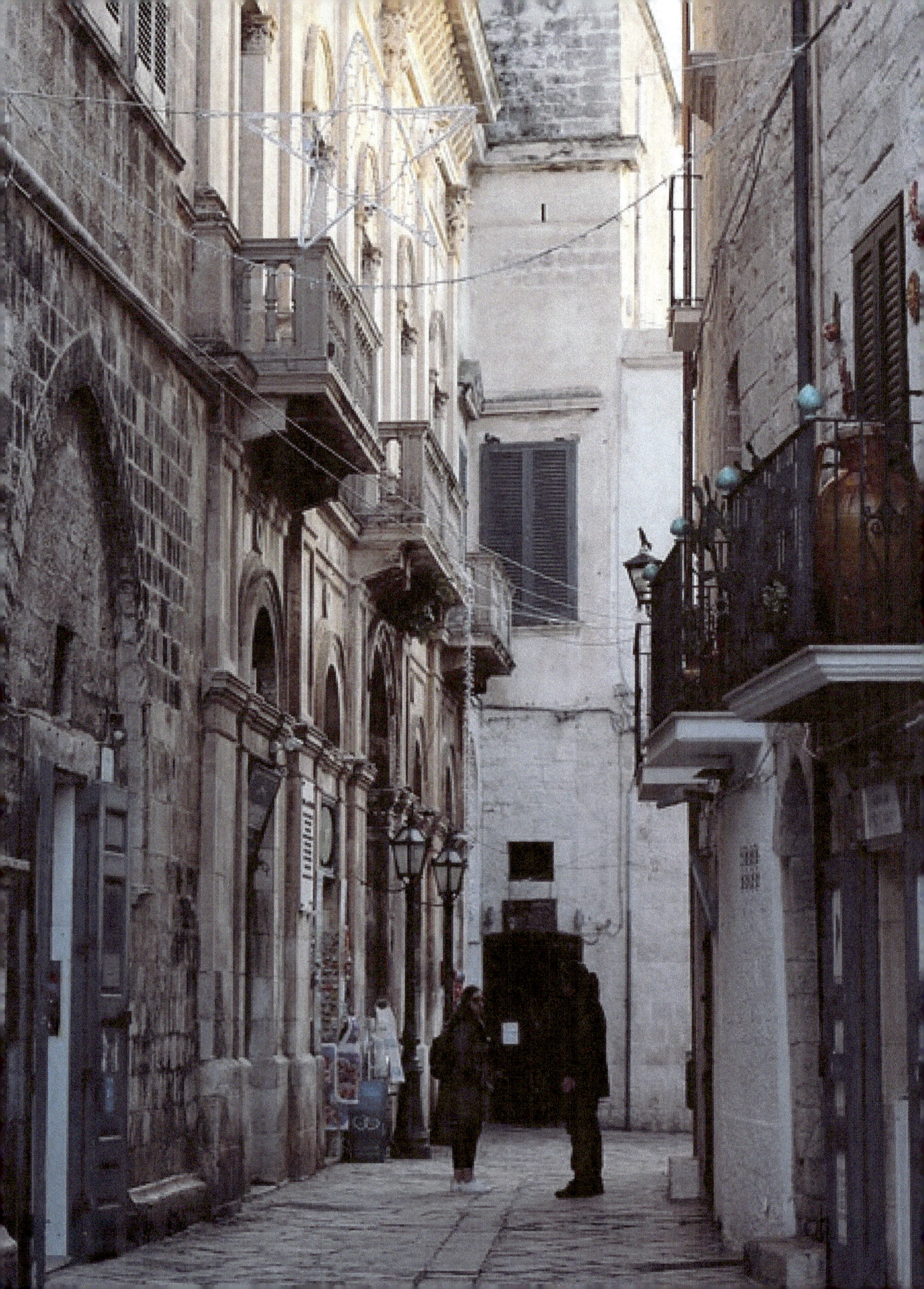

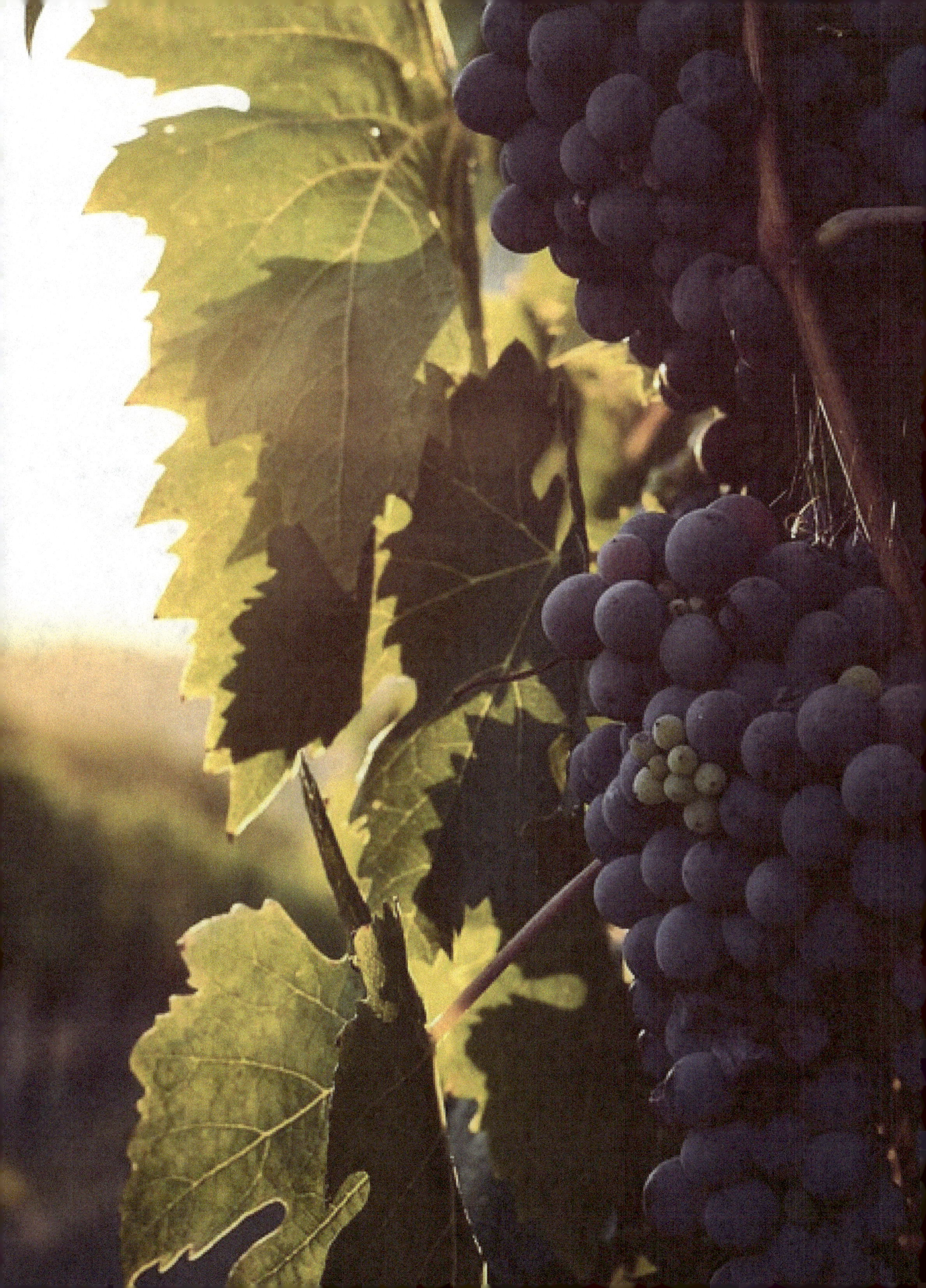

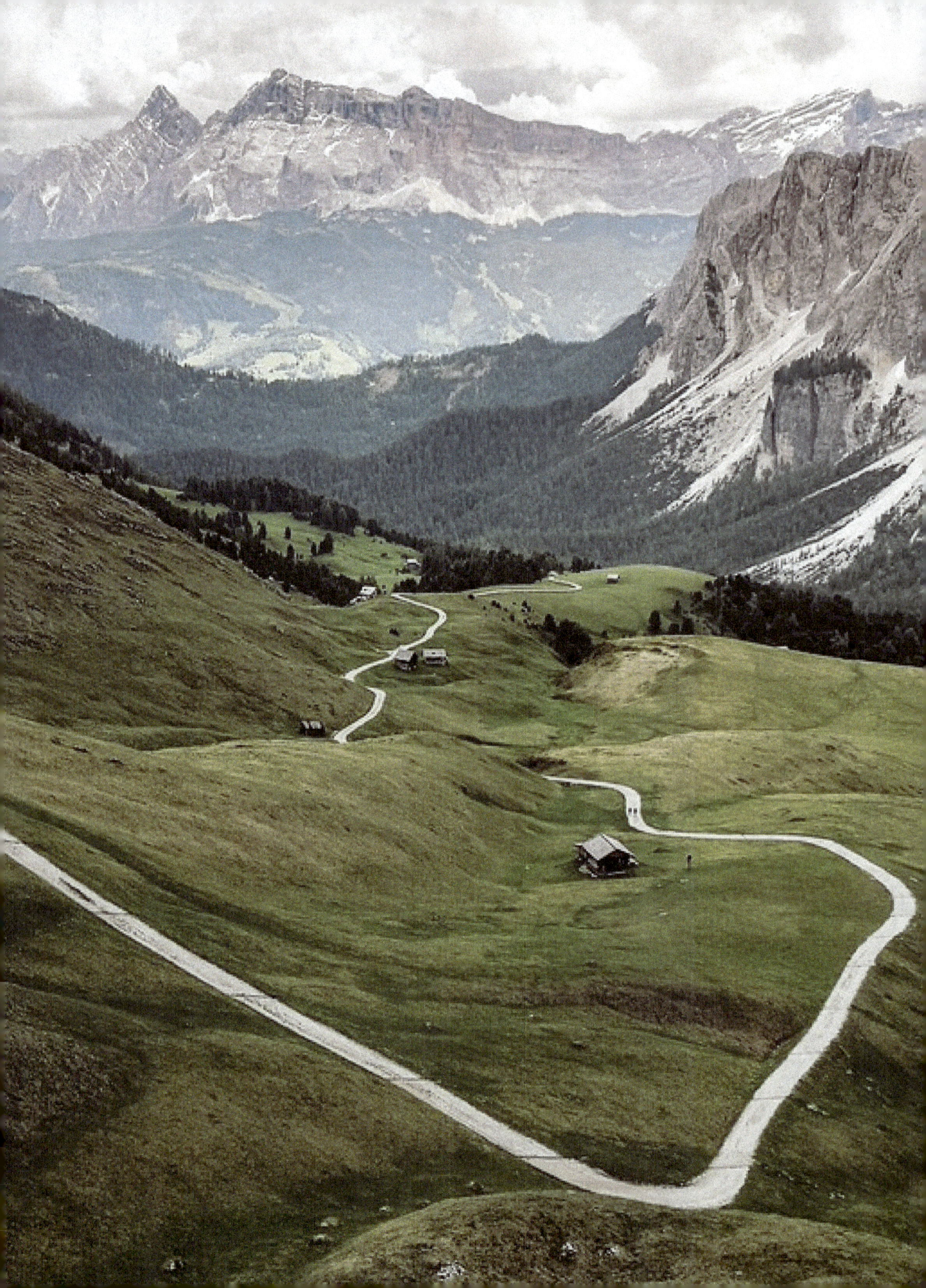

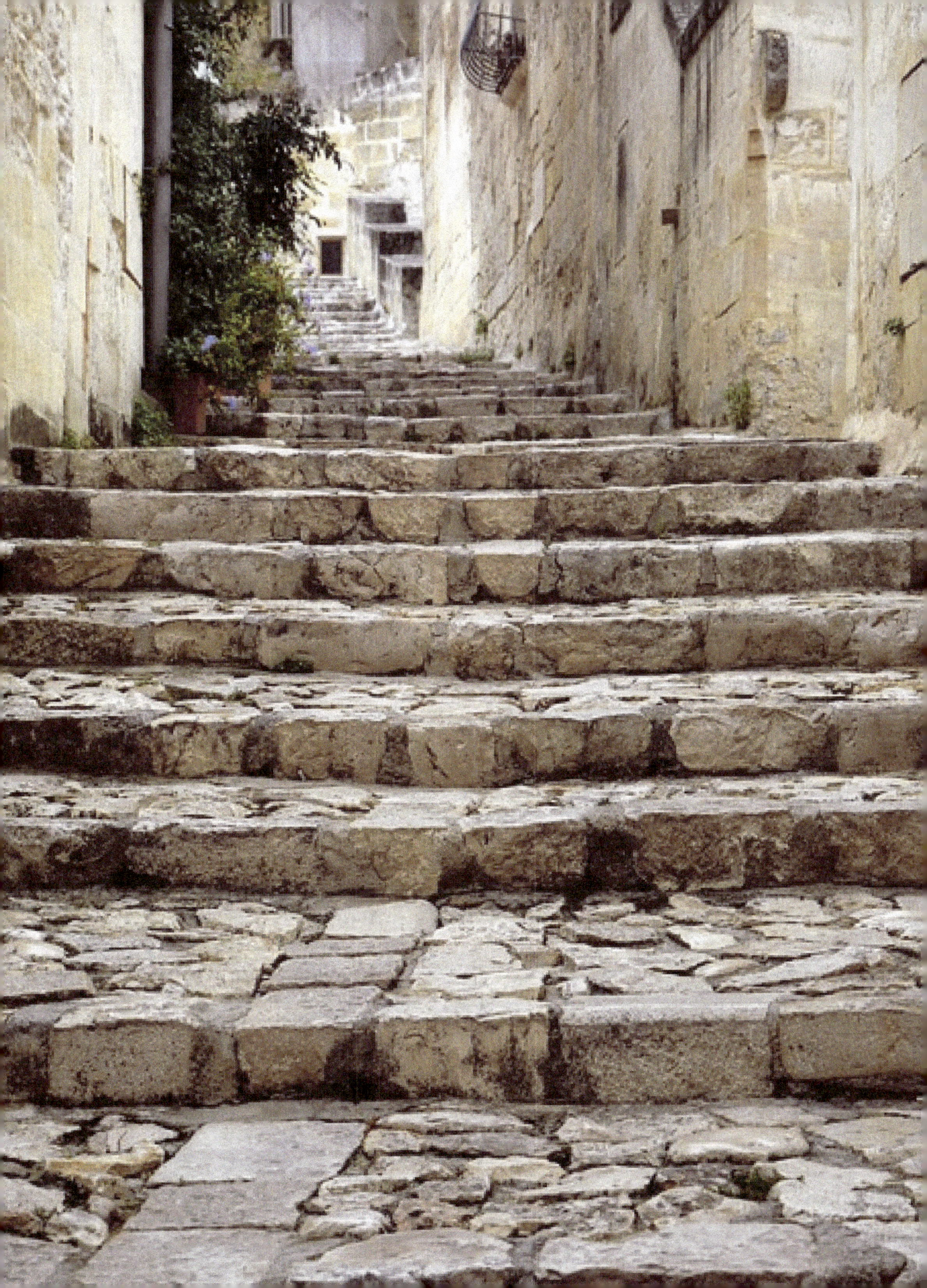

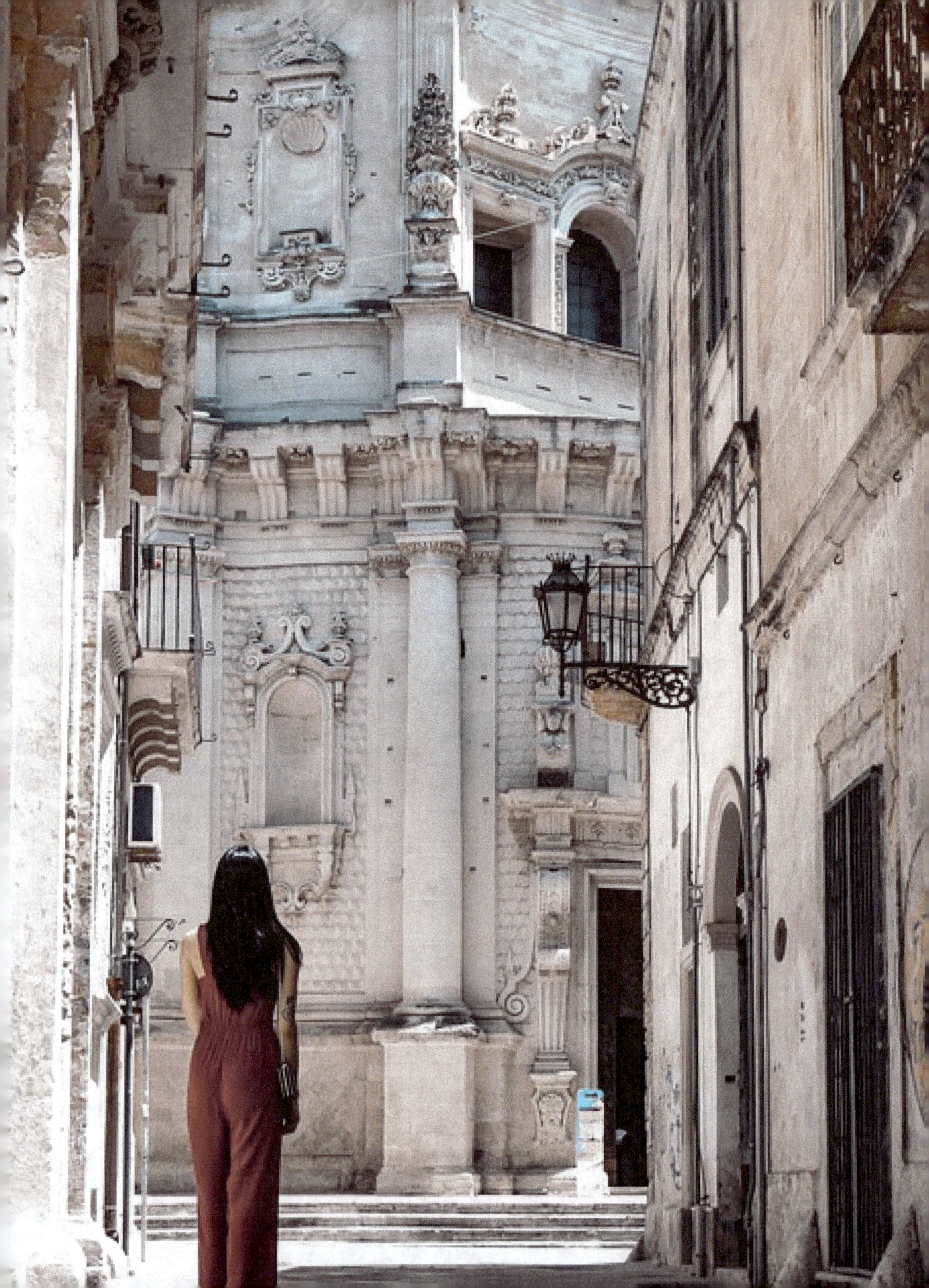

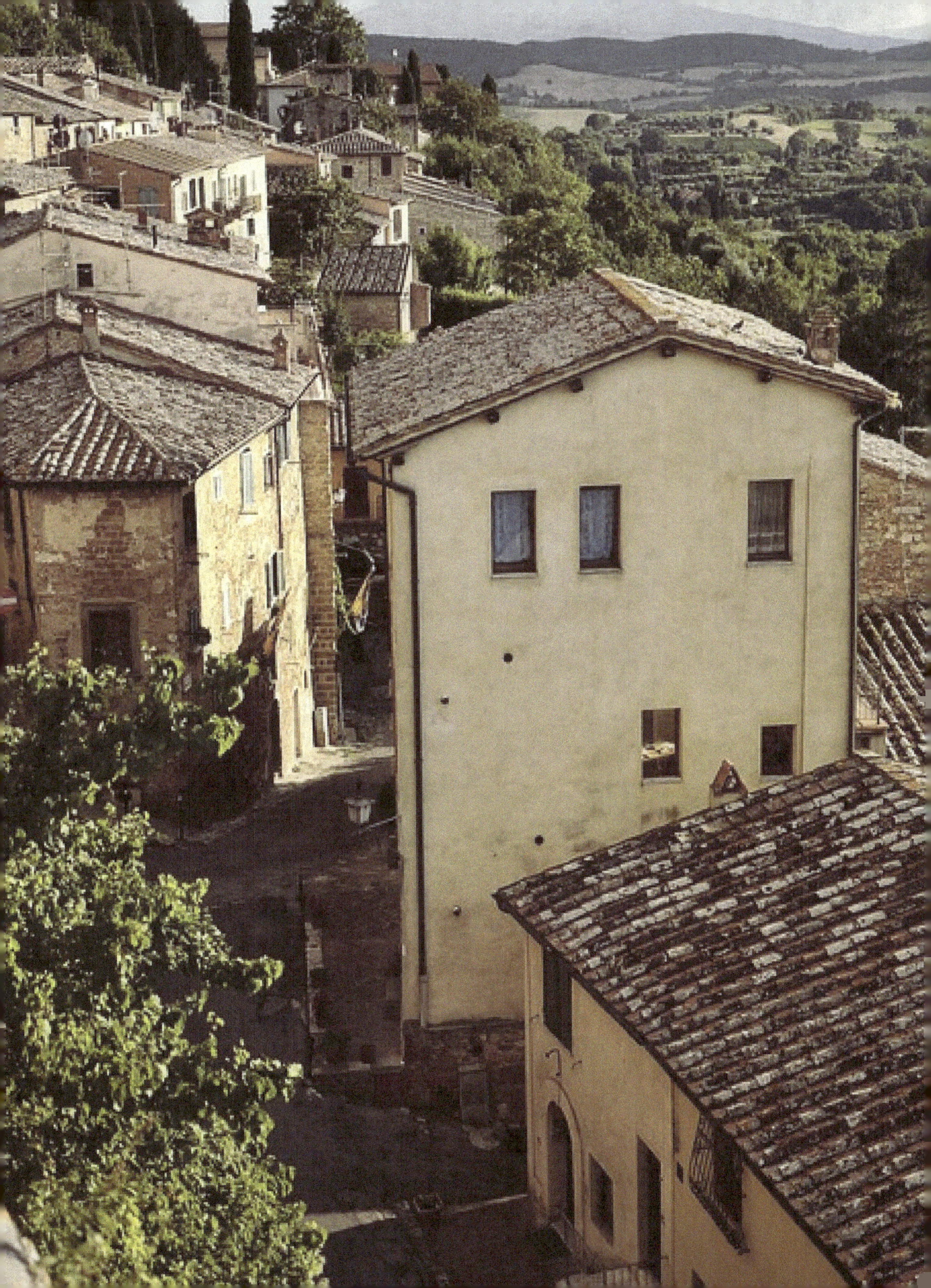

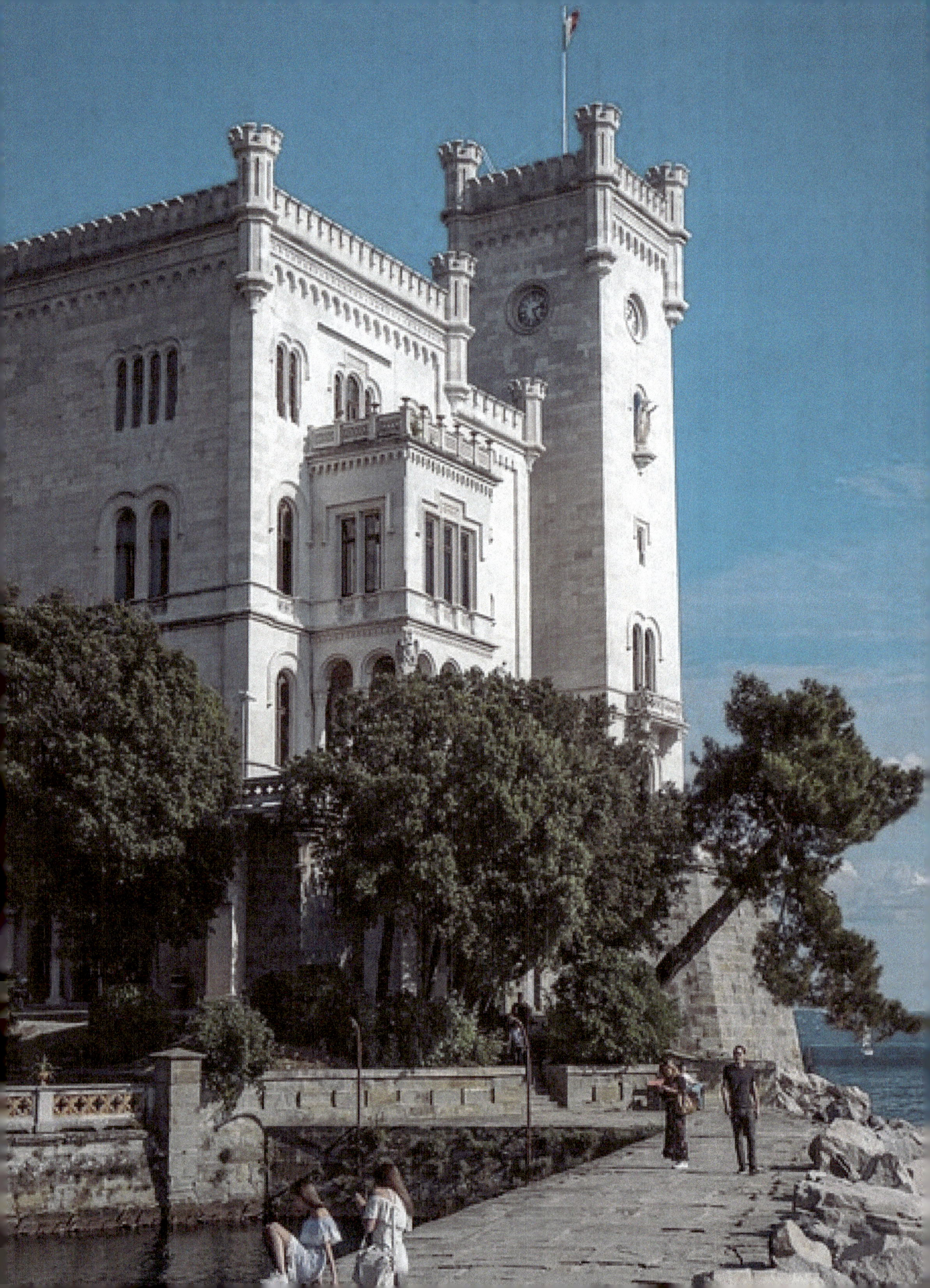

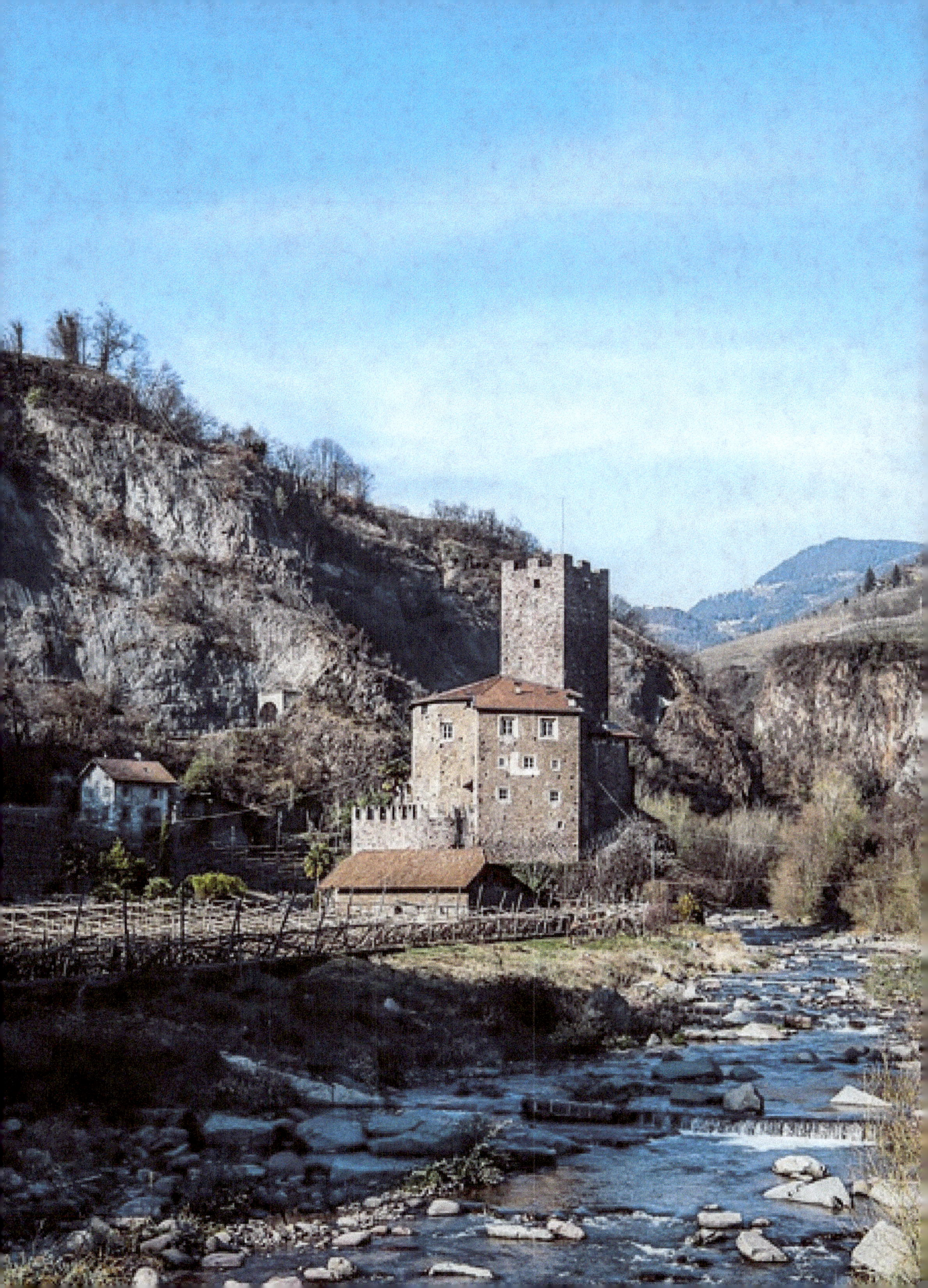

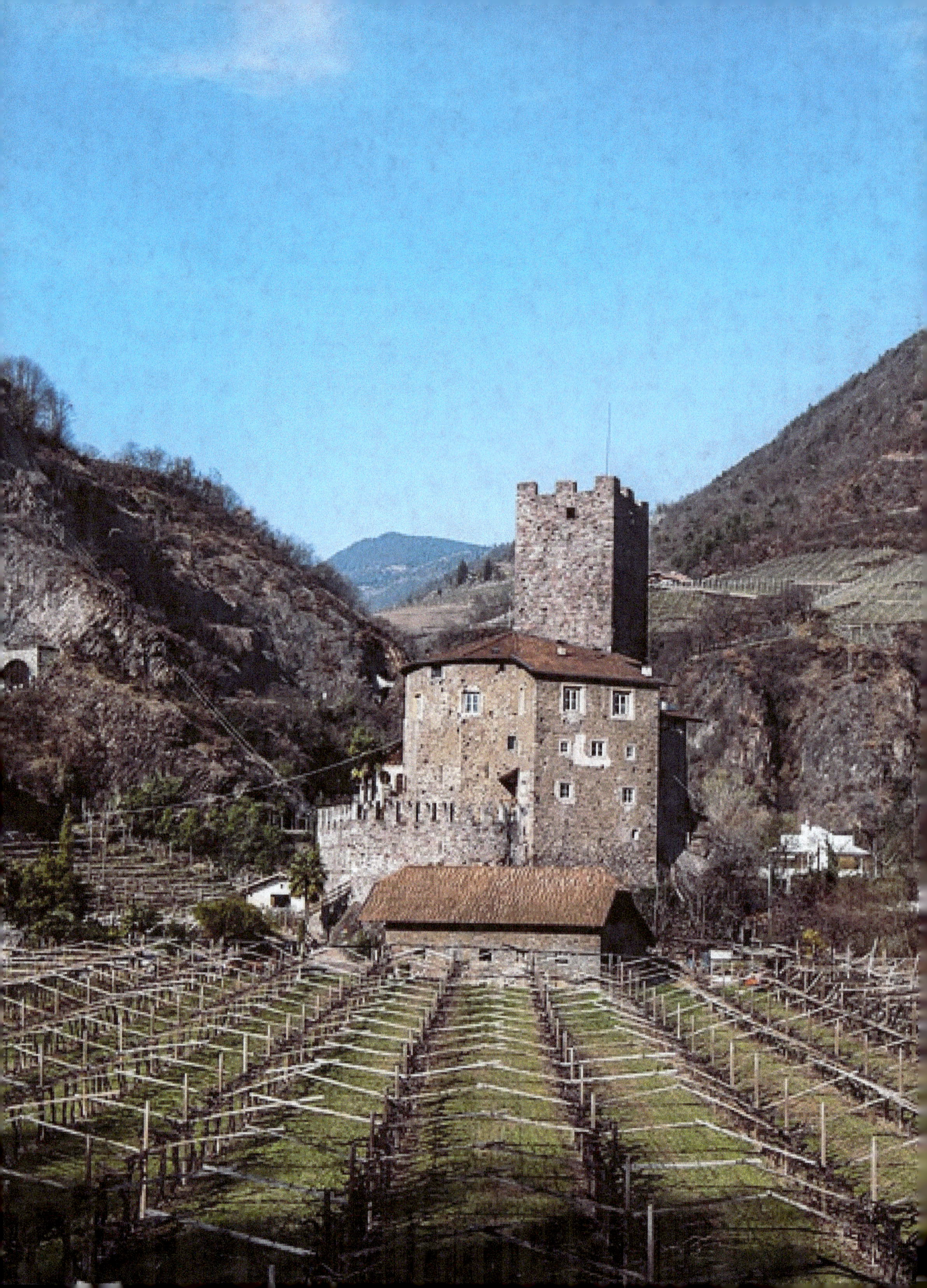

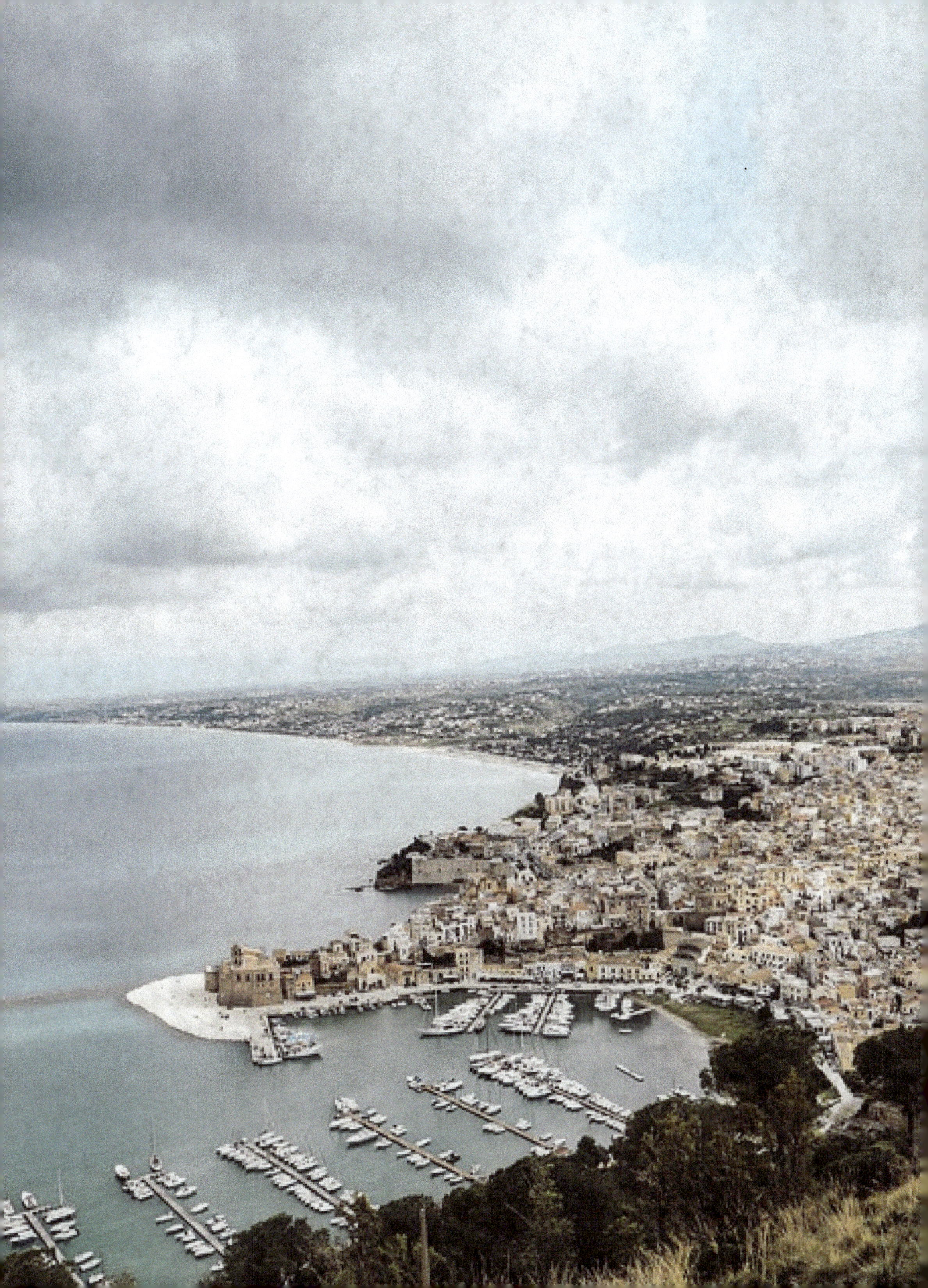

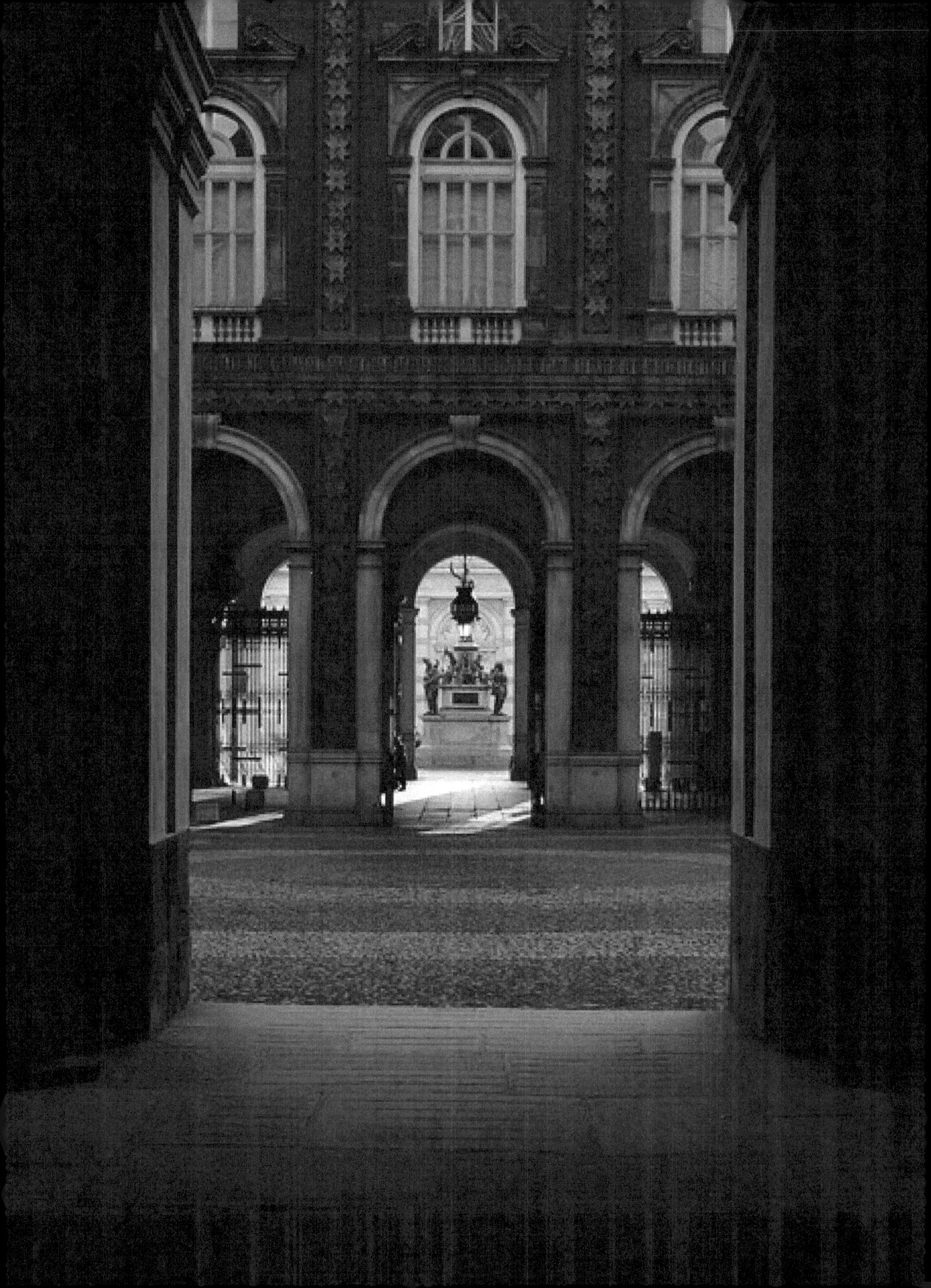

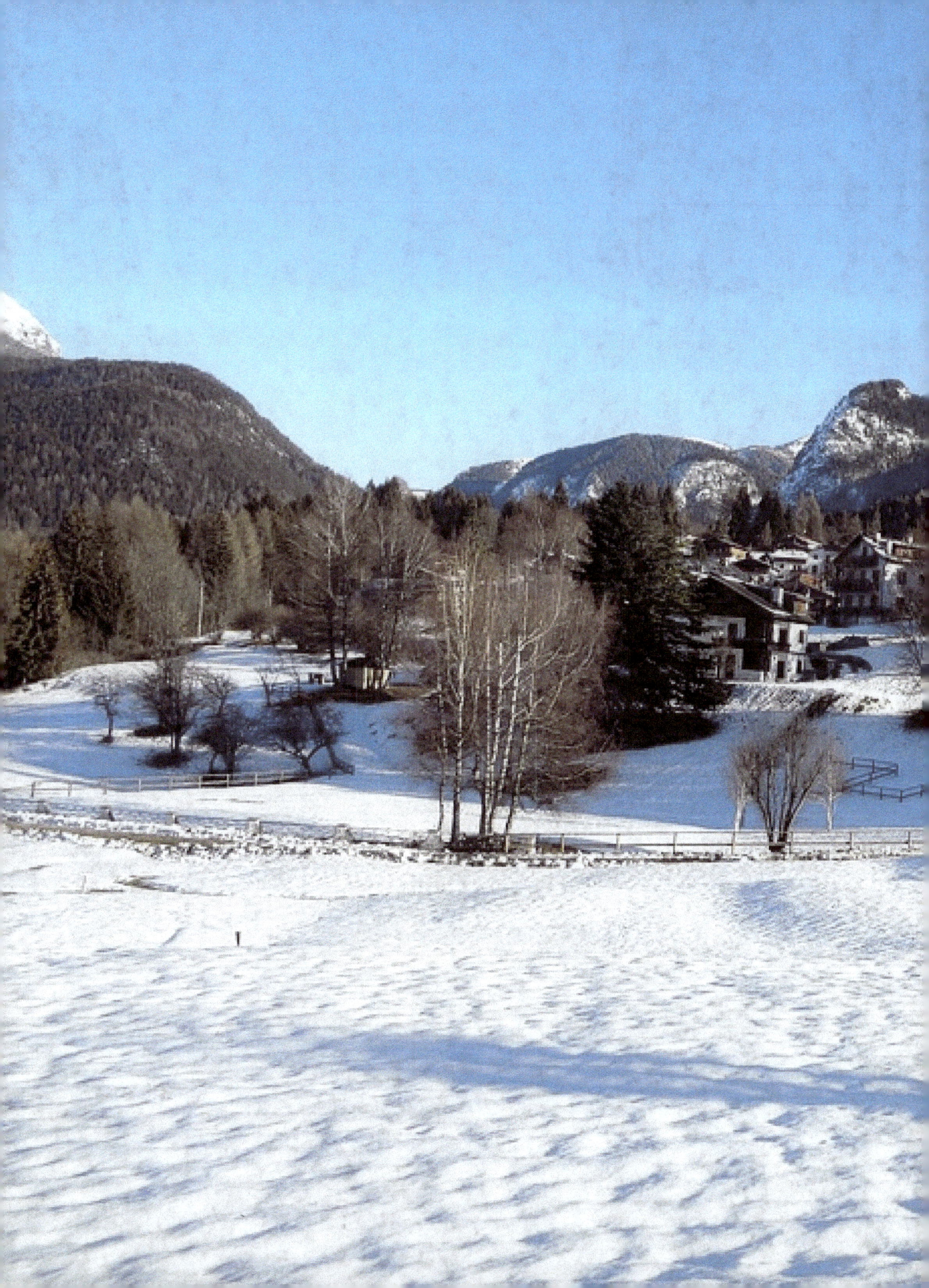

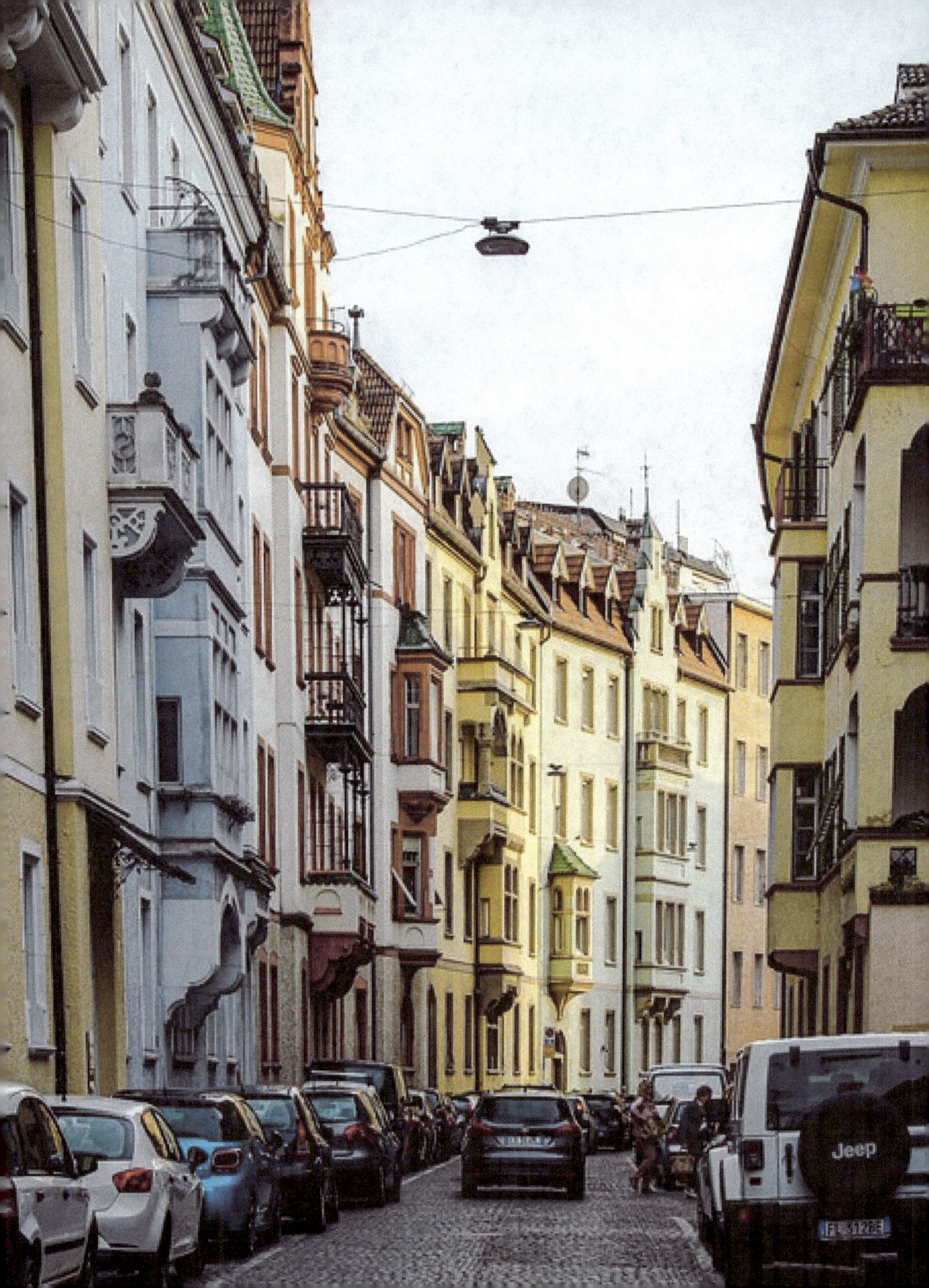
Jeep

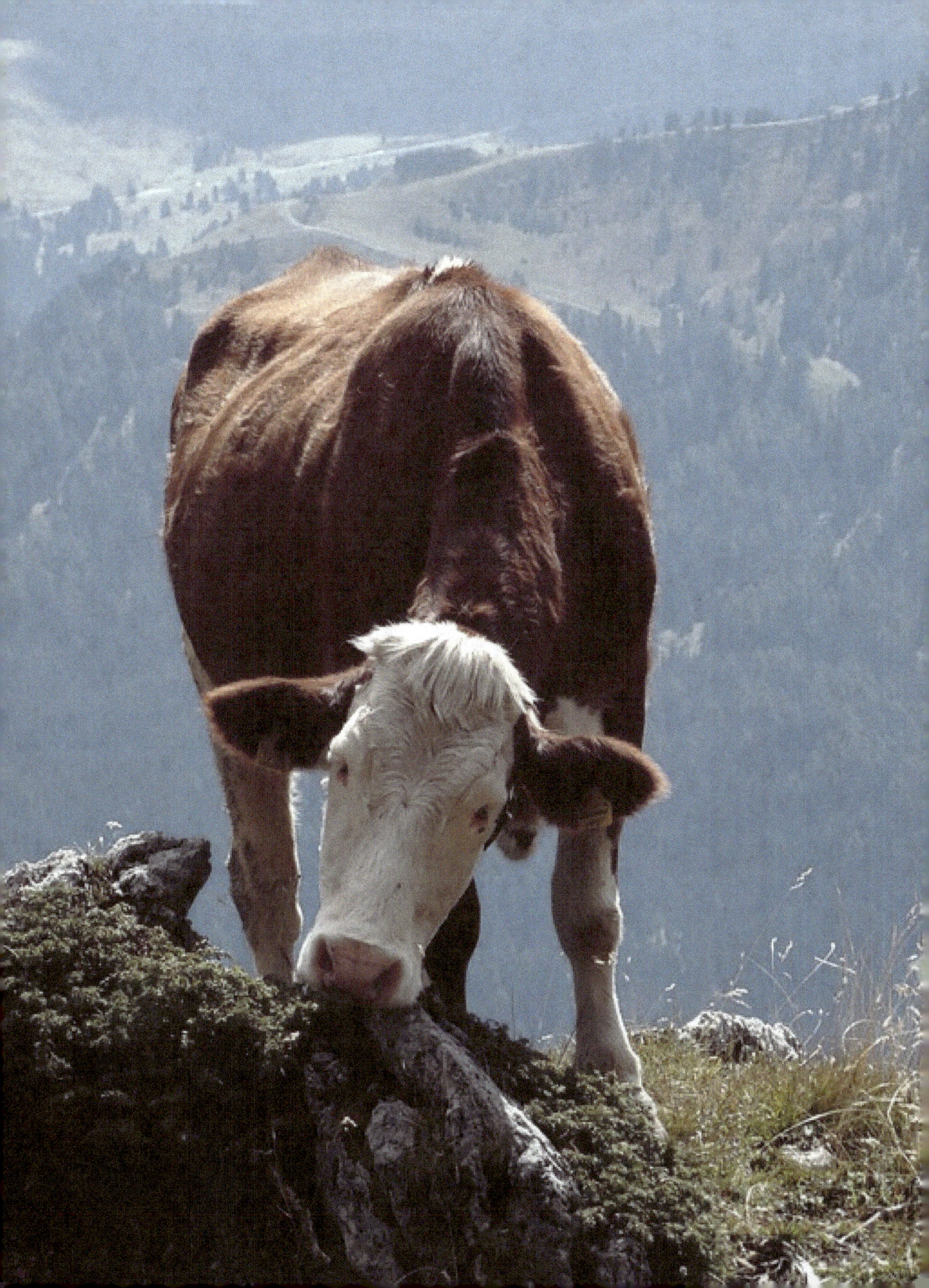

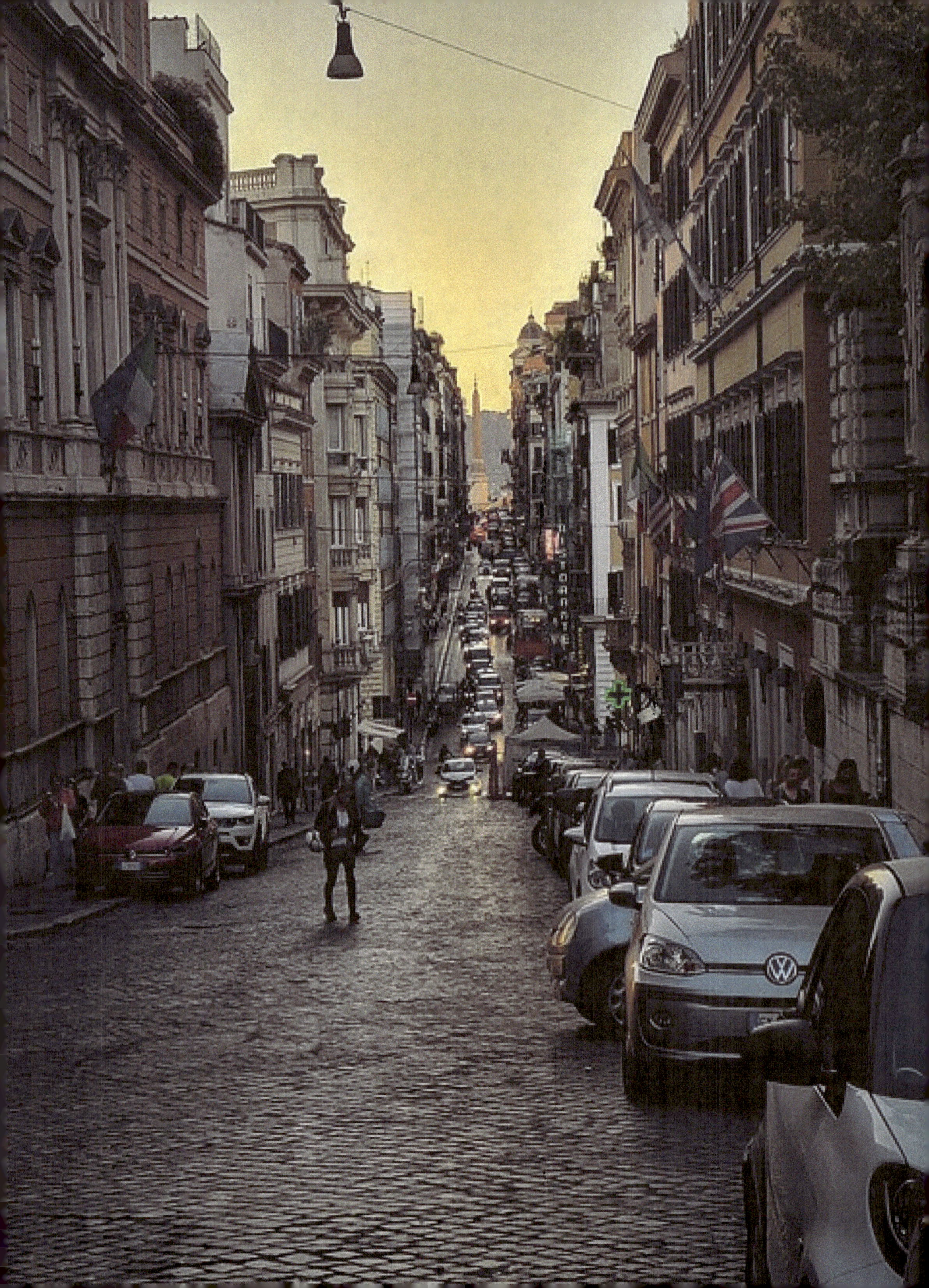

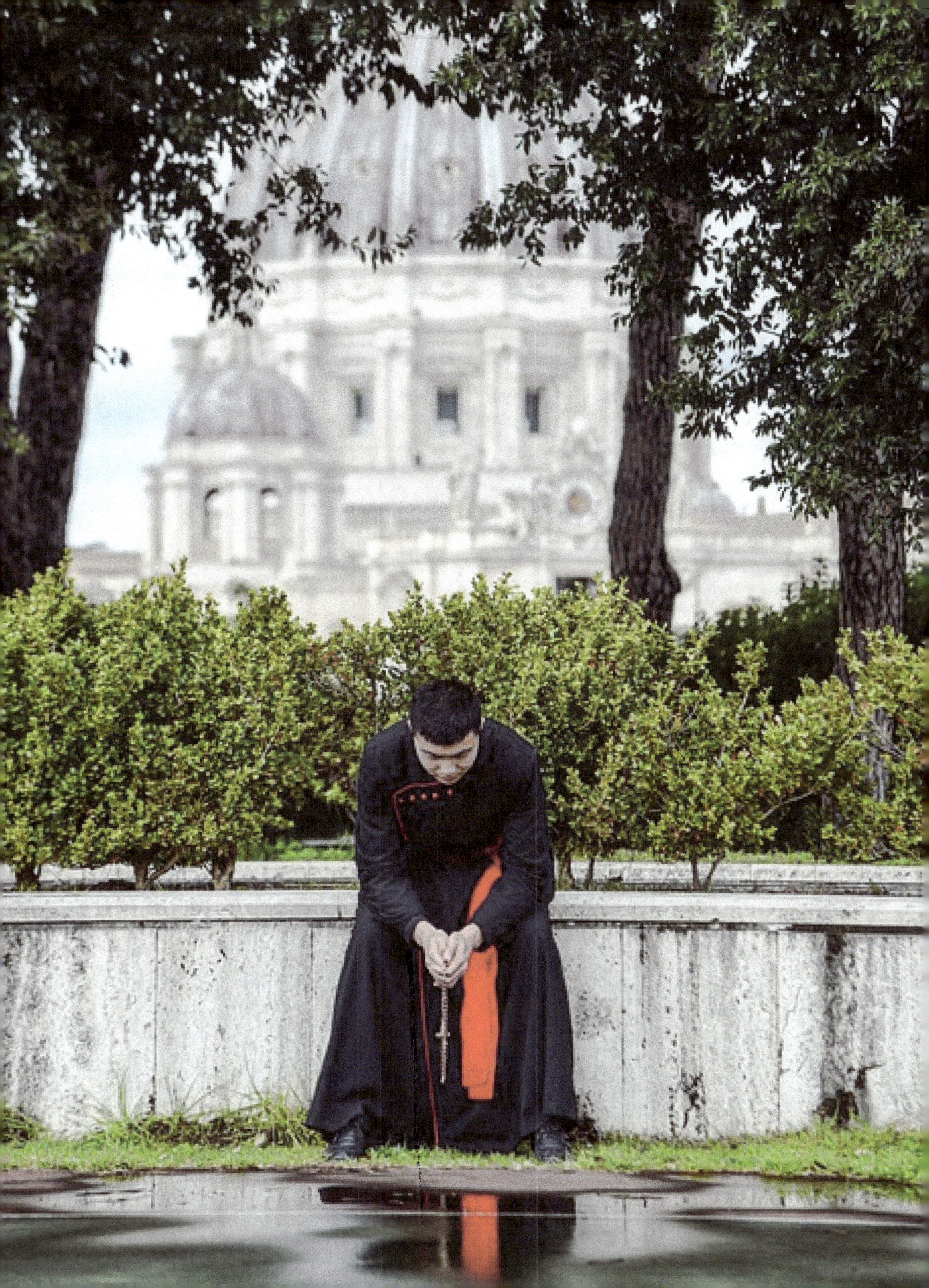

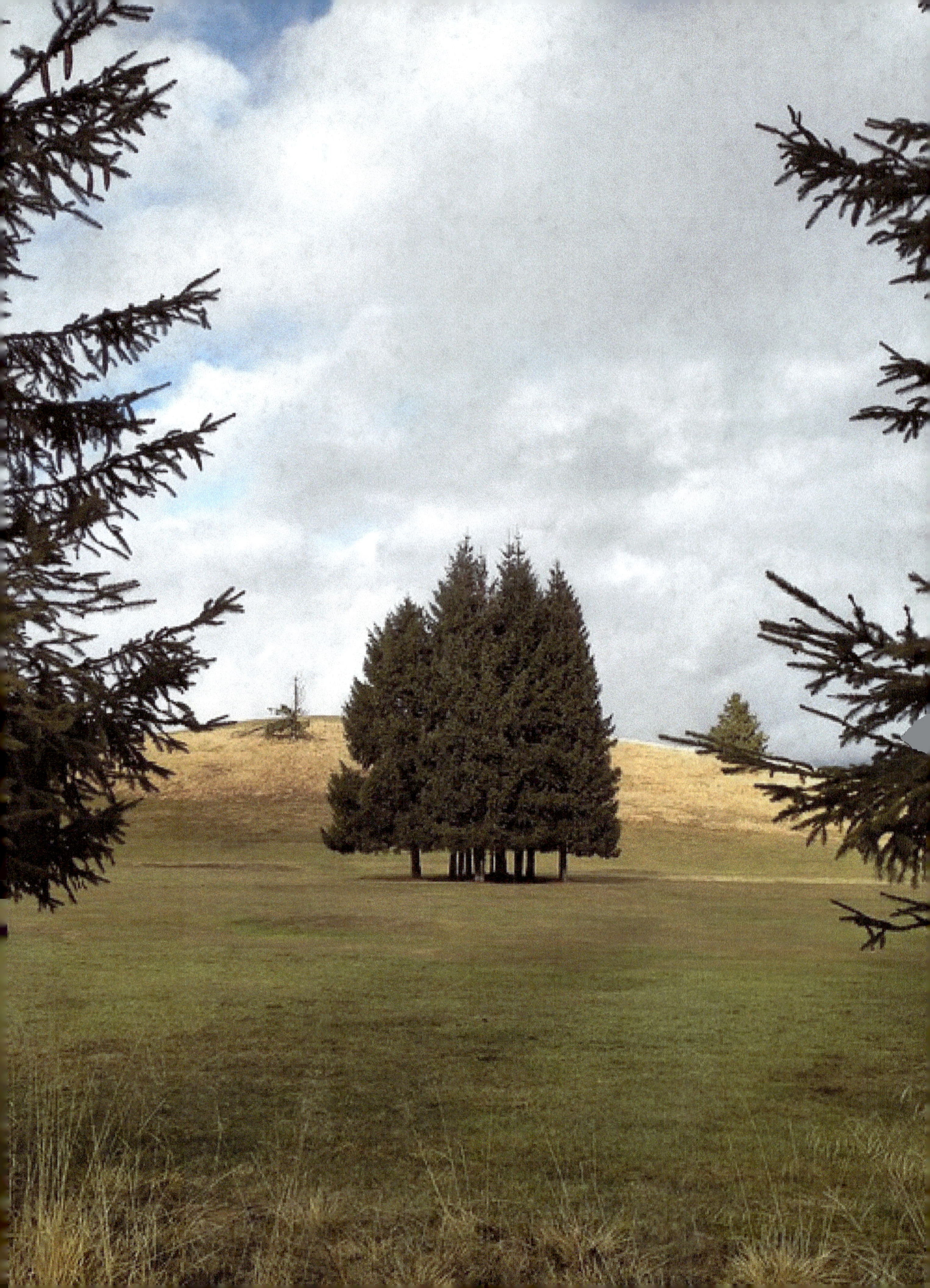

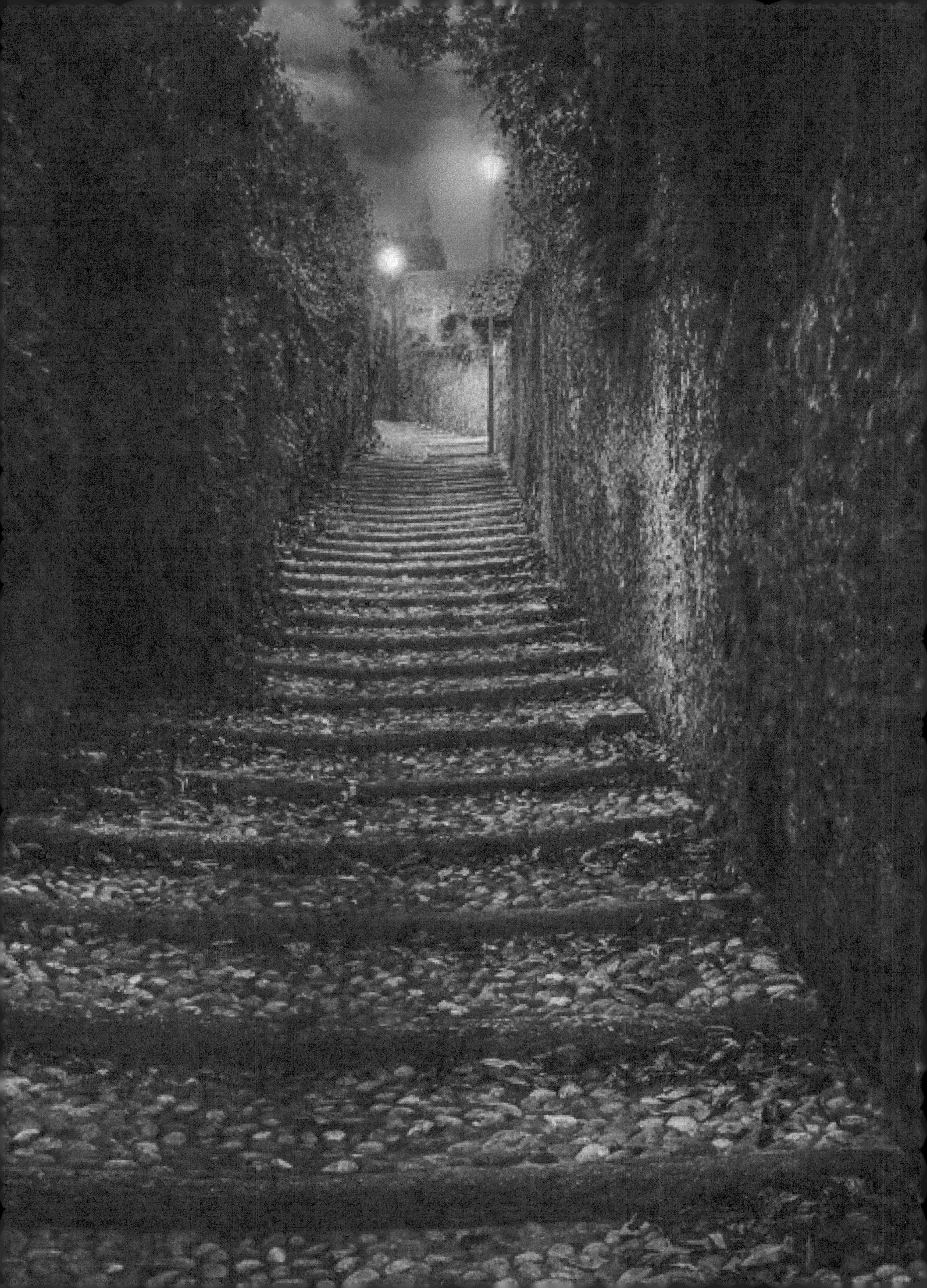

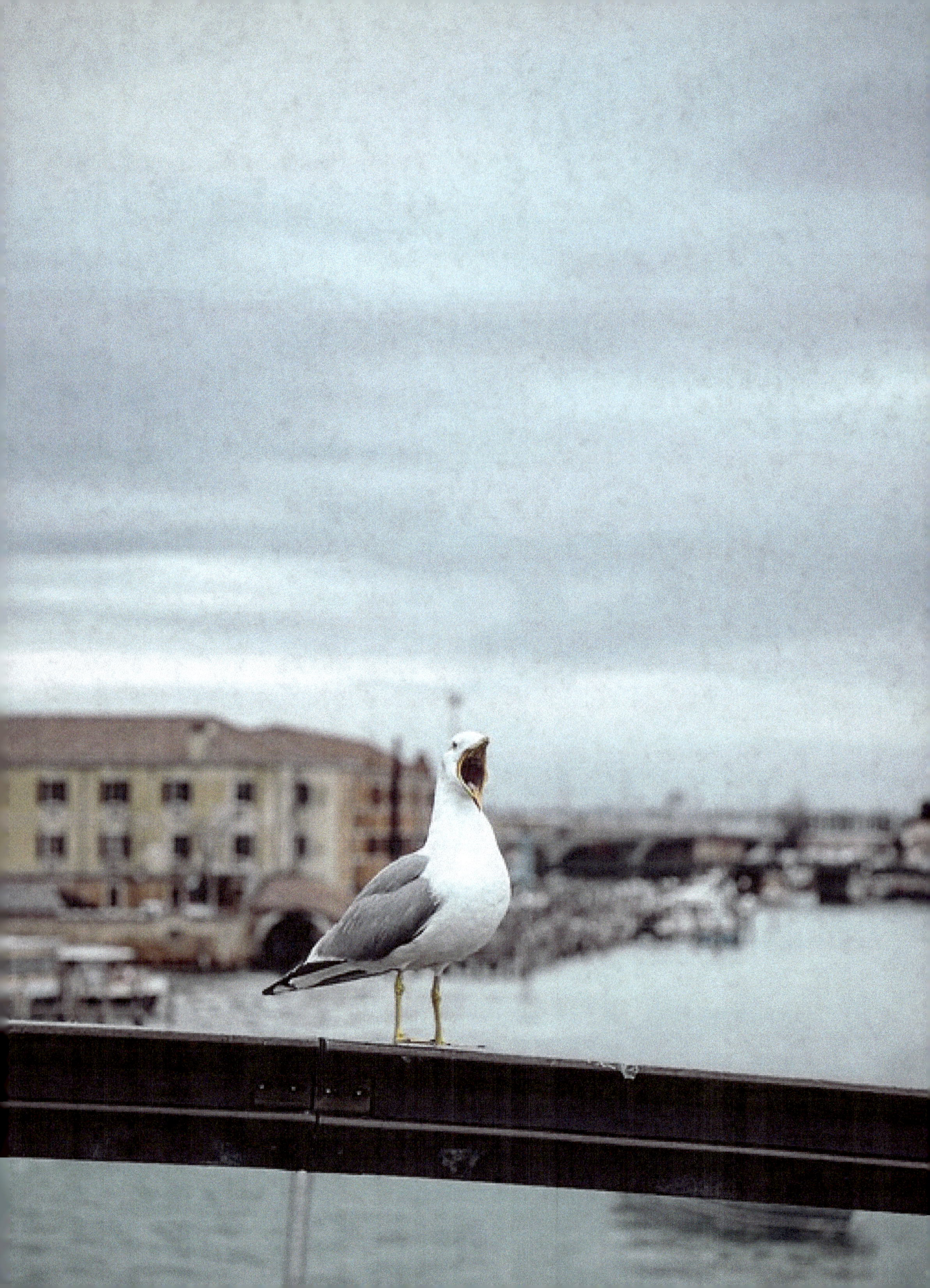

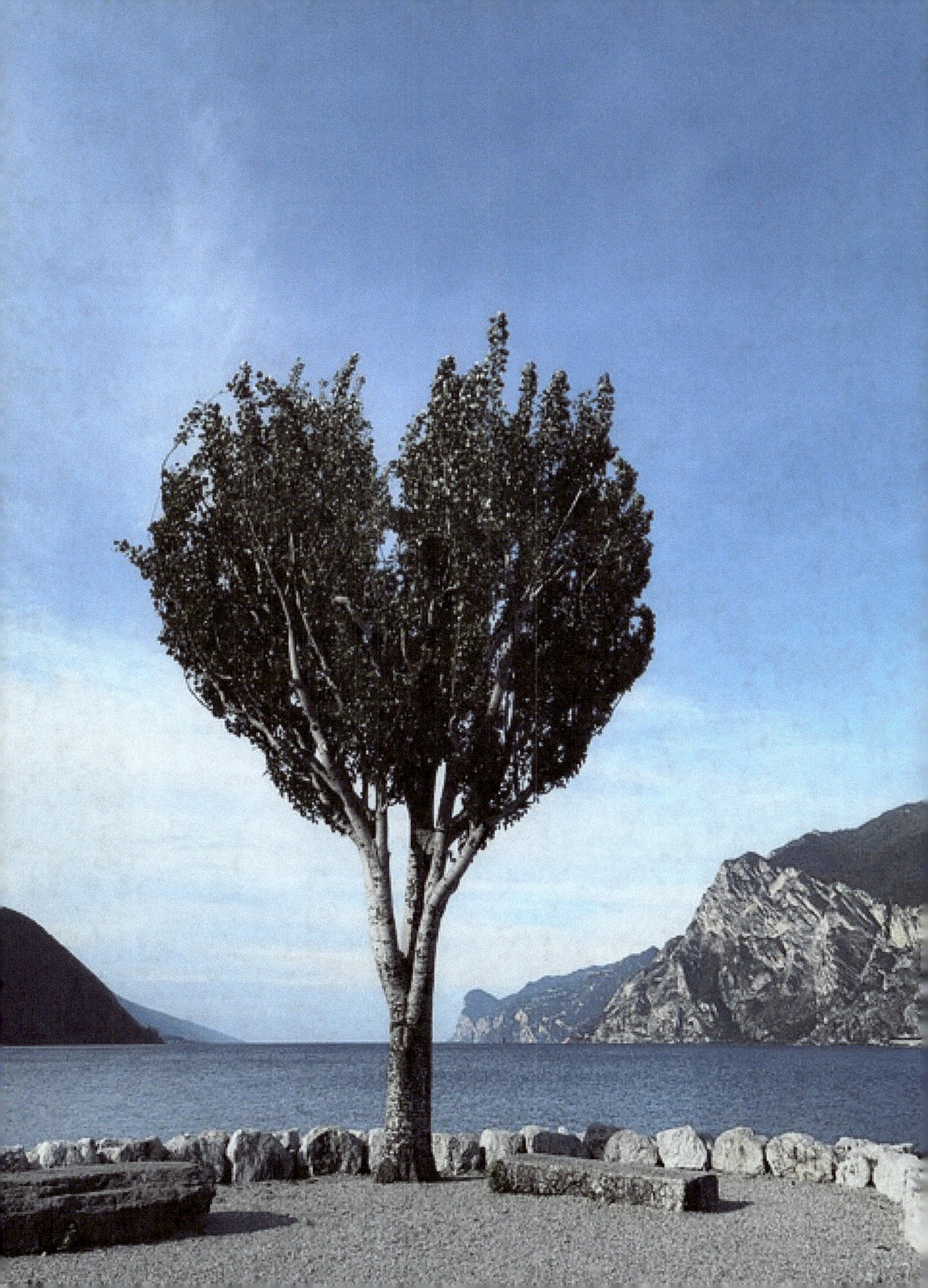

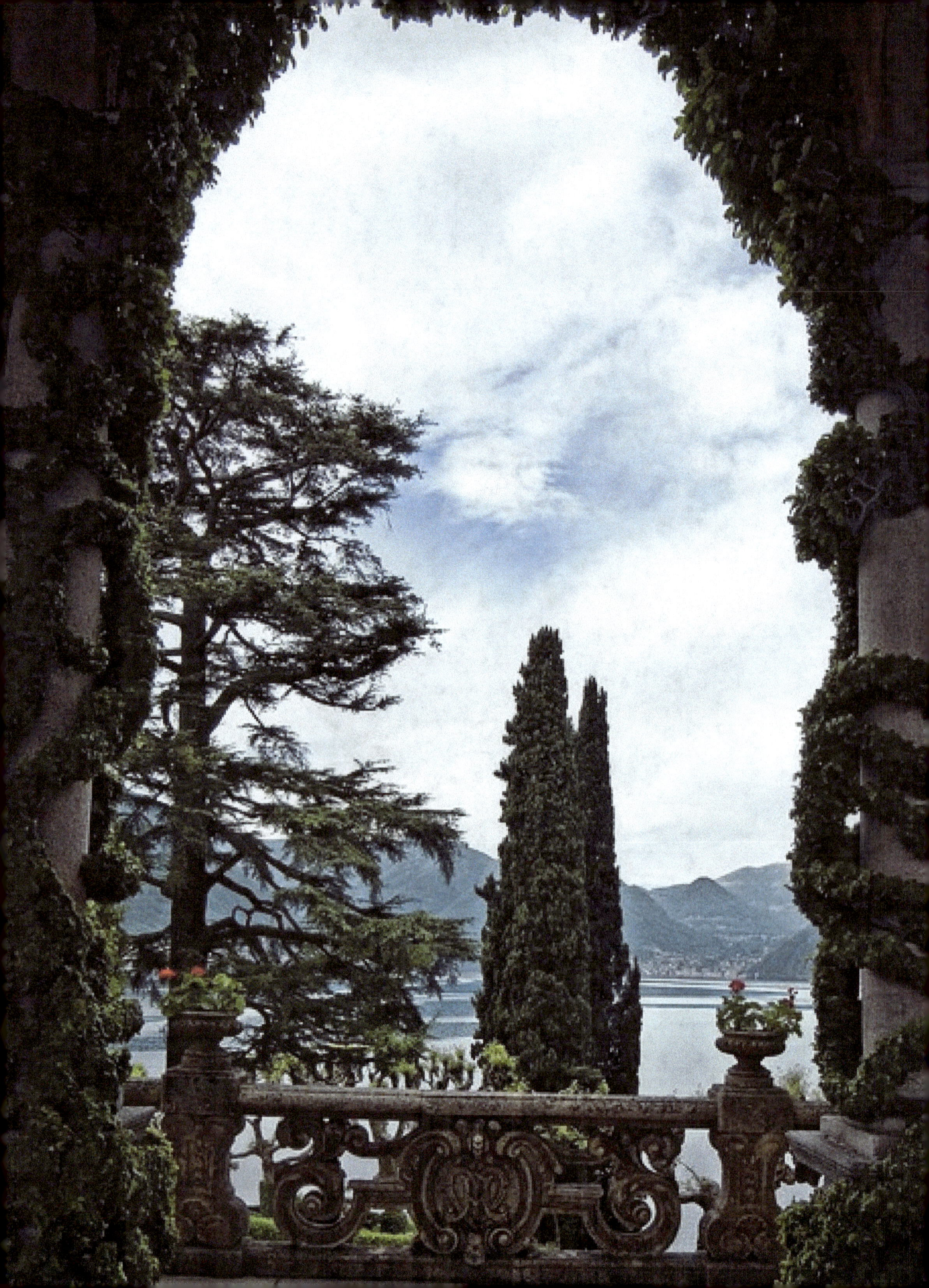

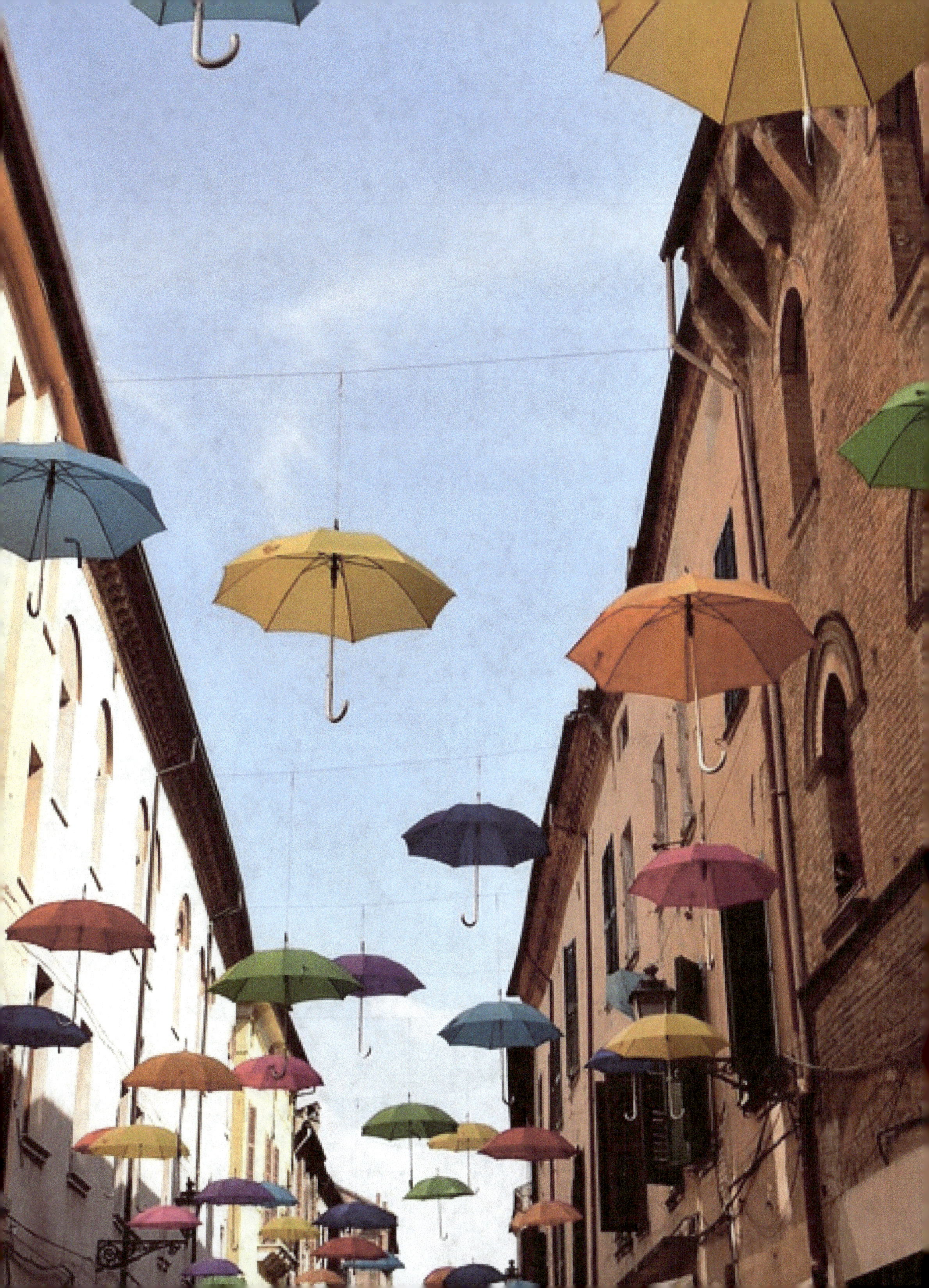

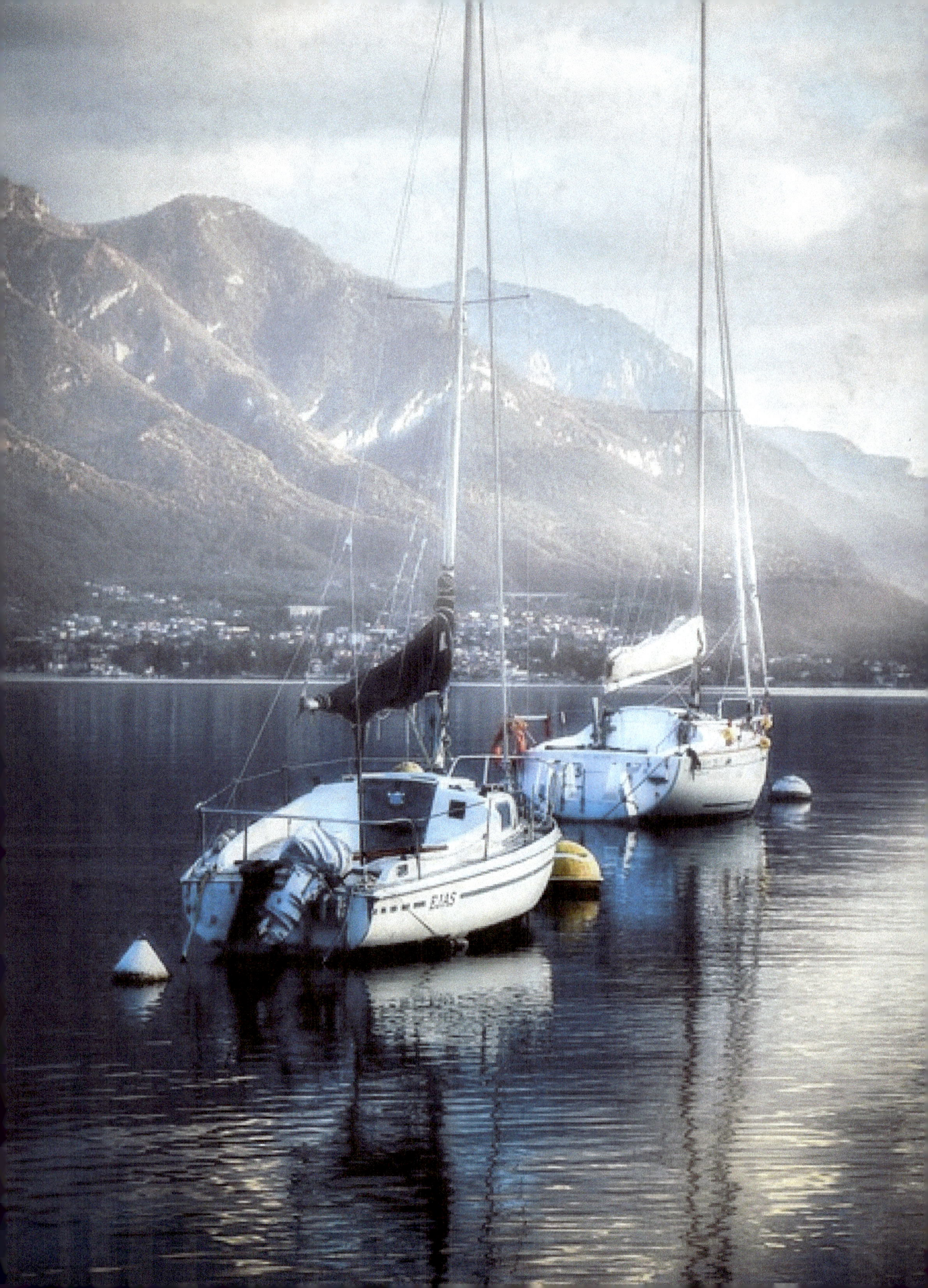

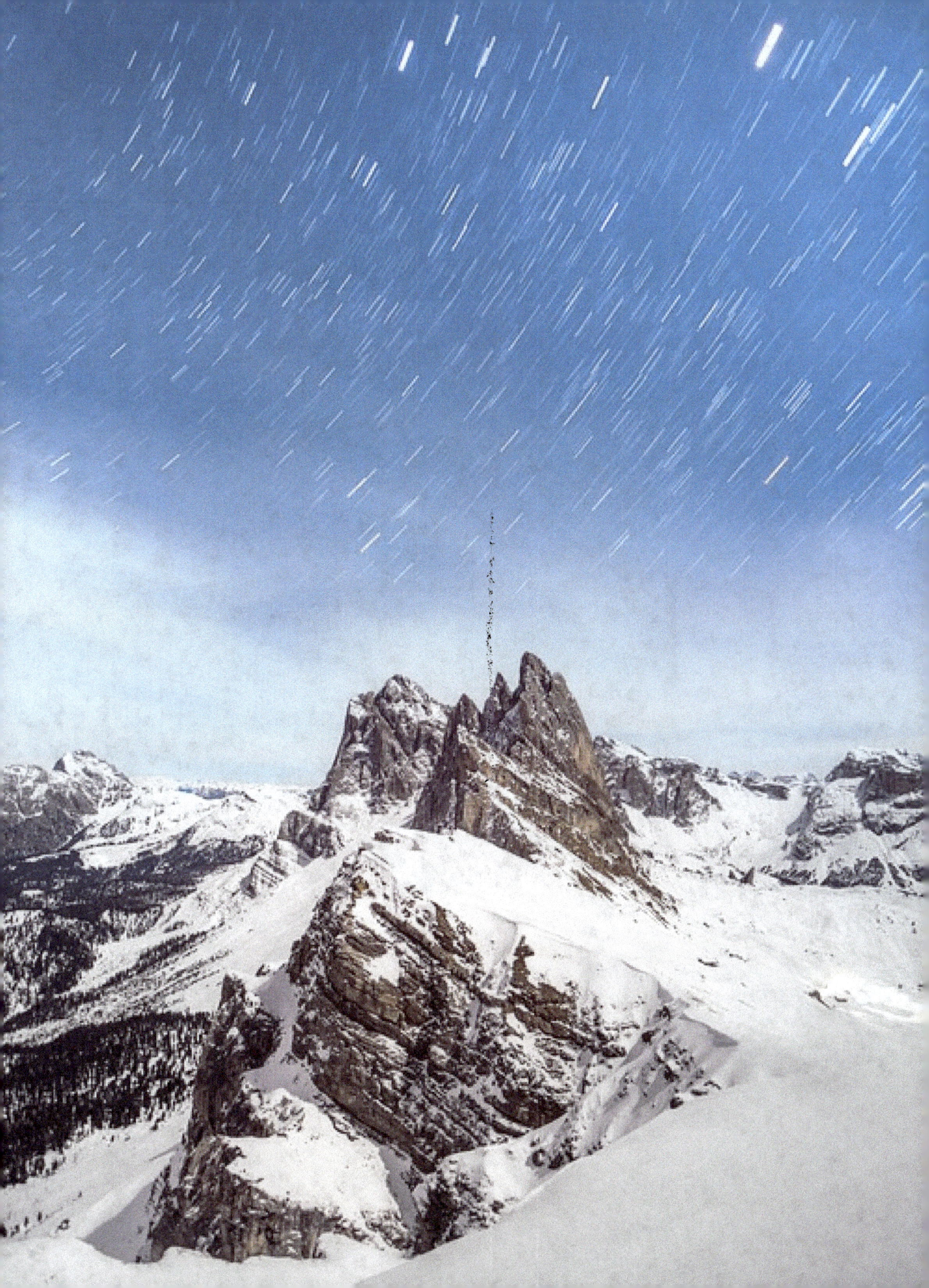

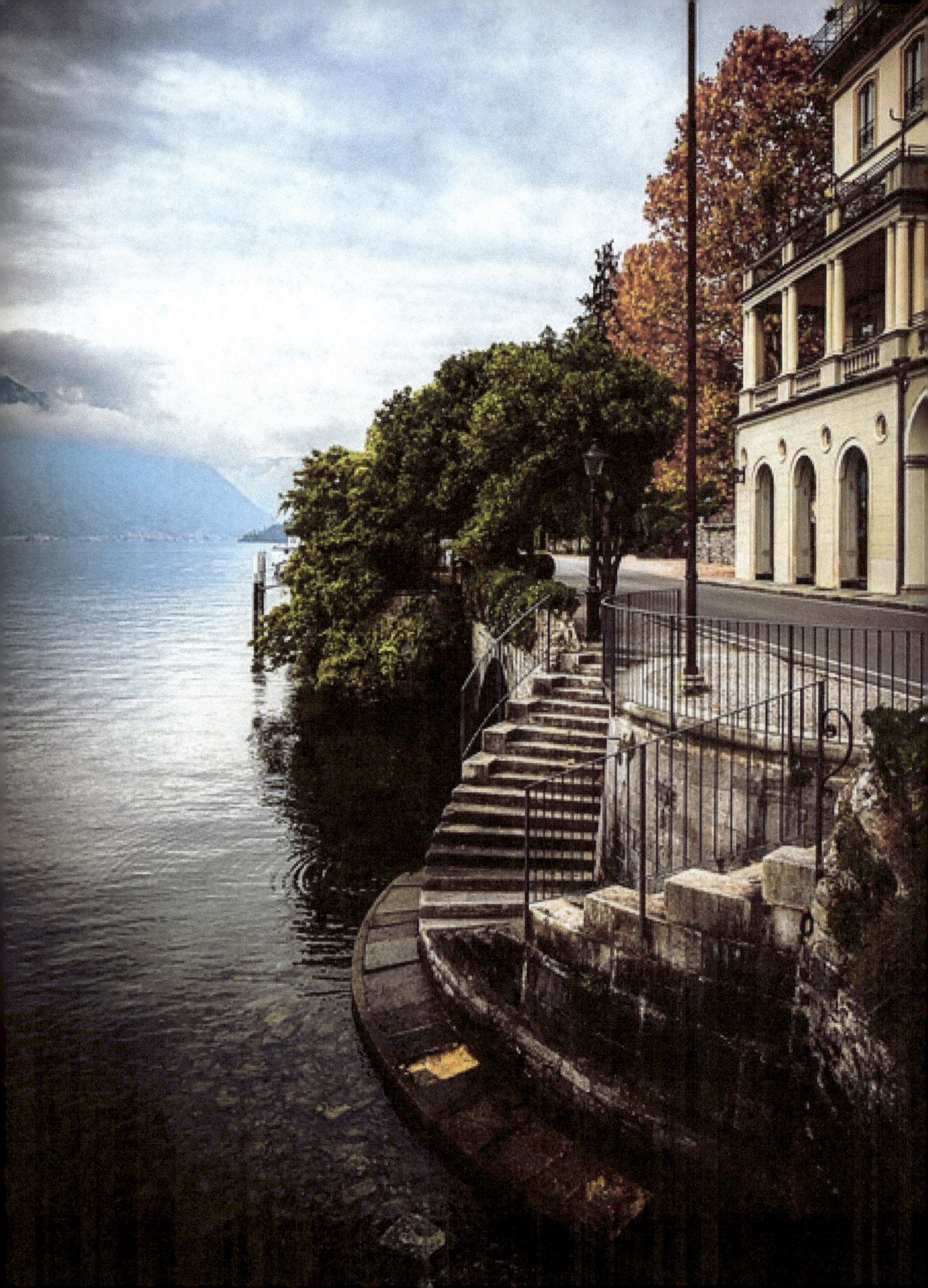

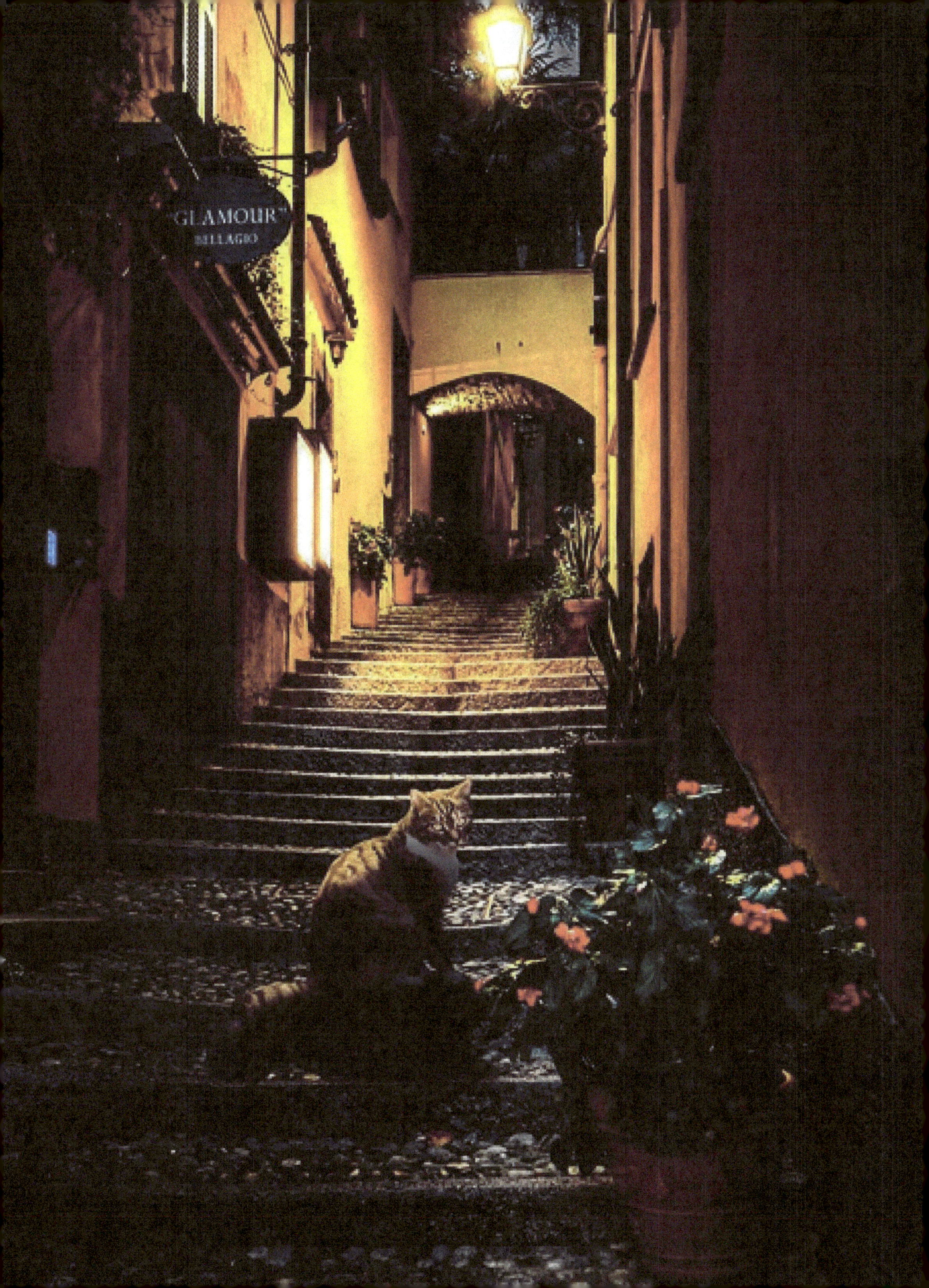
"GLAMOUR"
BELLAGIO

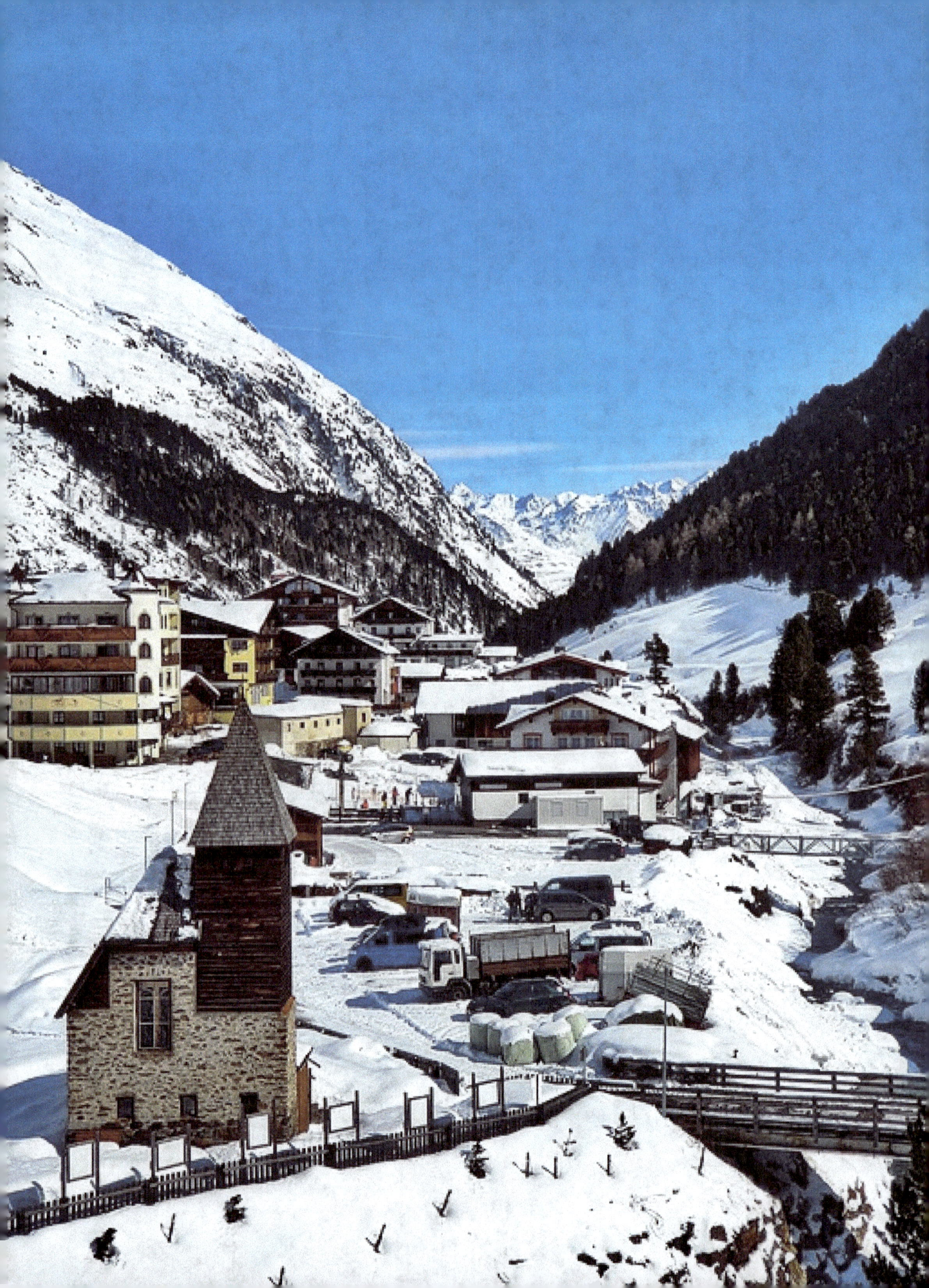

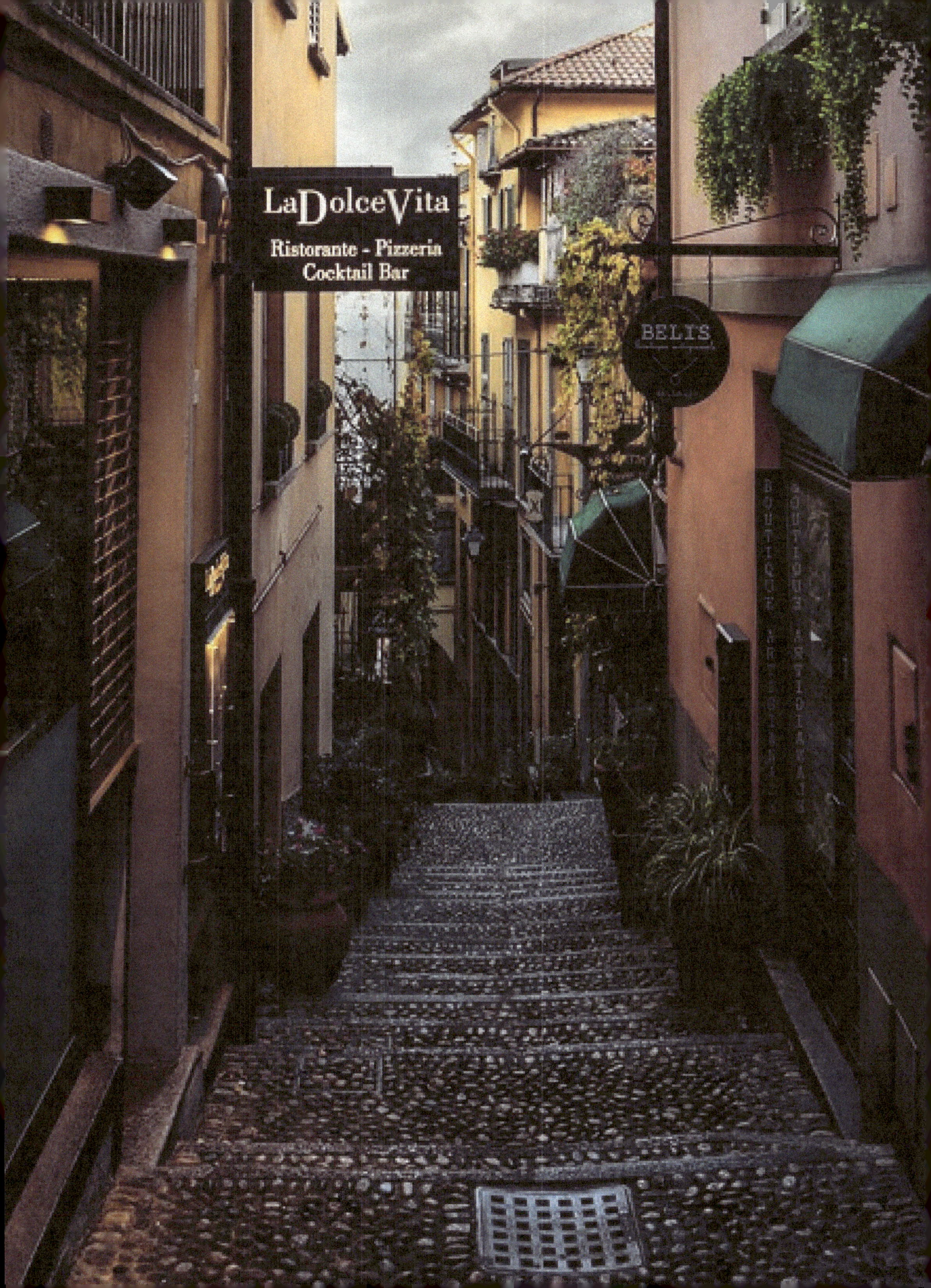
LaDolceVita
Ristorante - Pizzeria
Cocktail Bar
BELIS

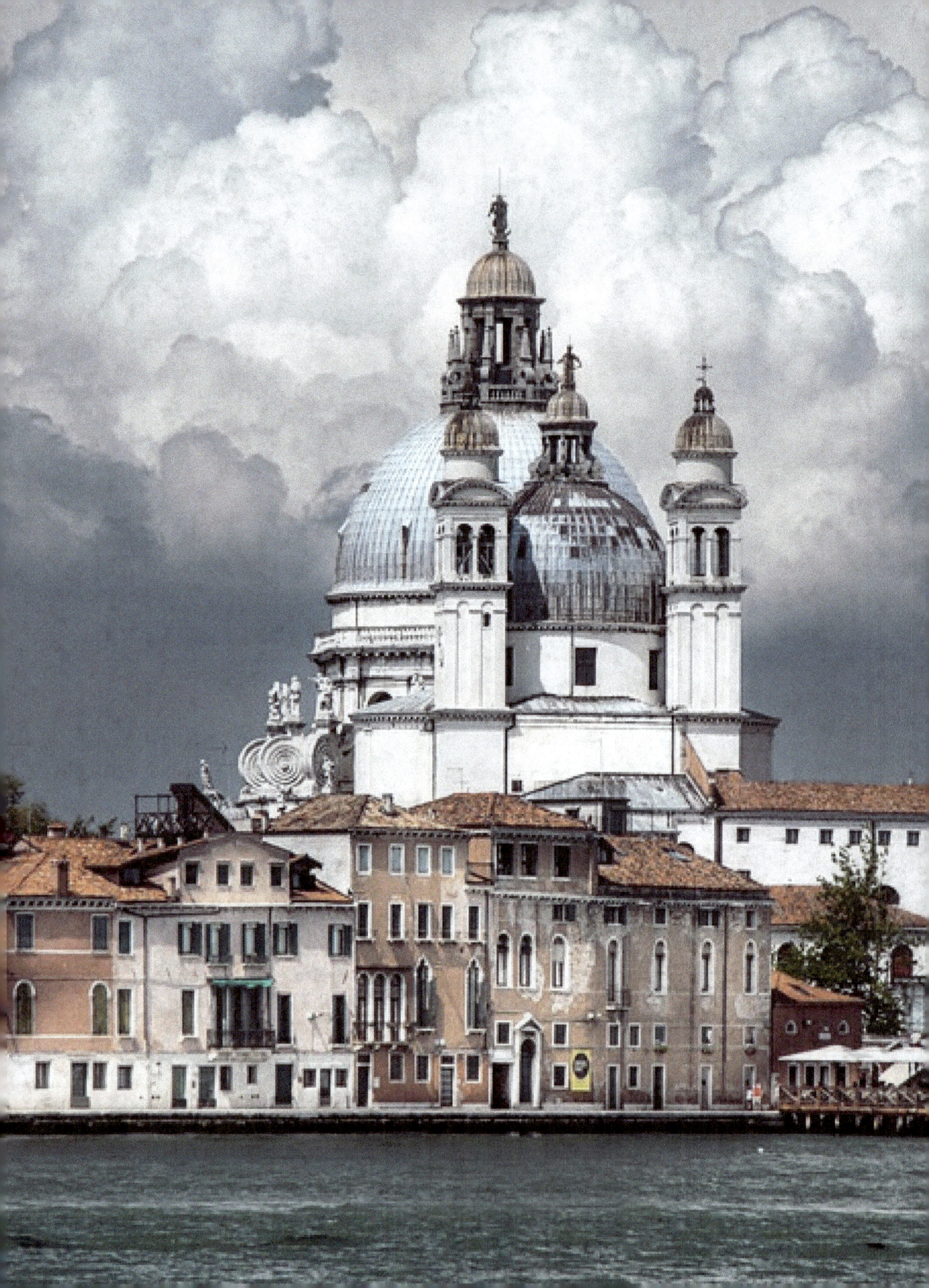

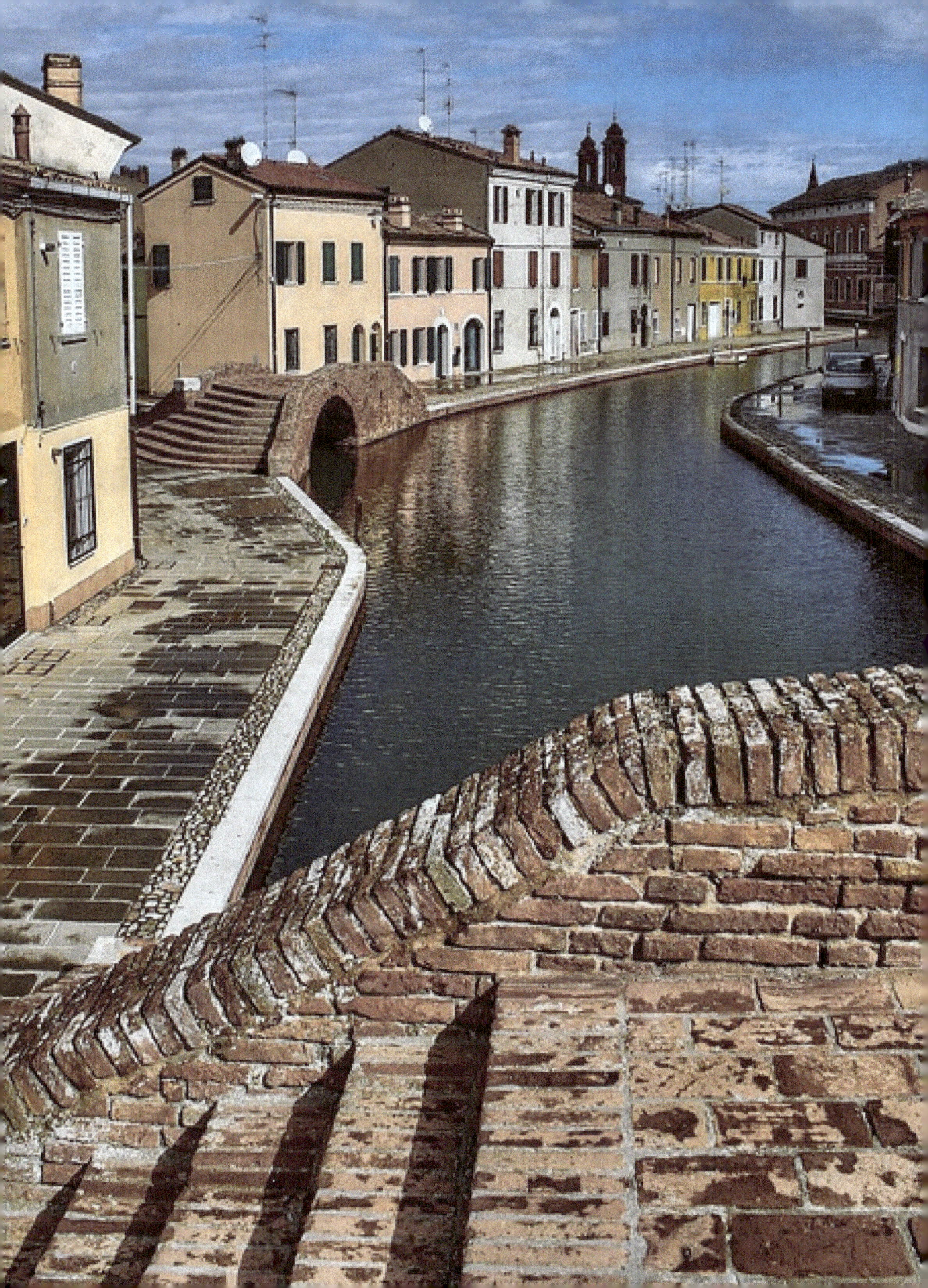

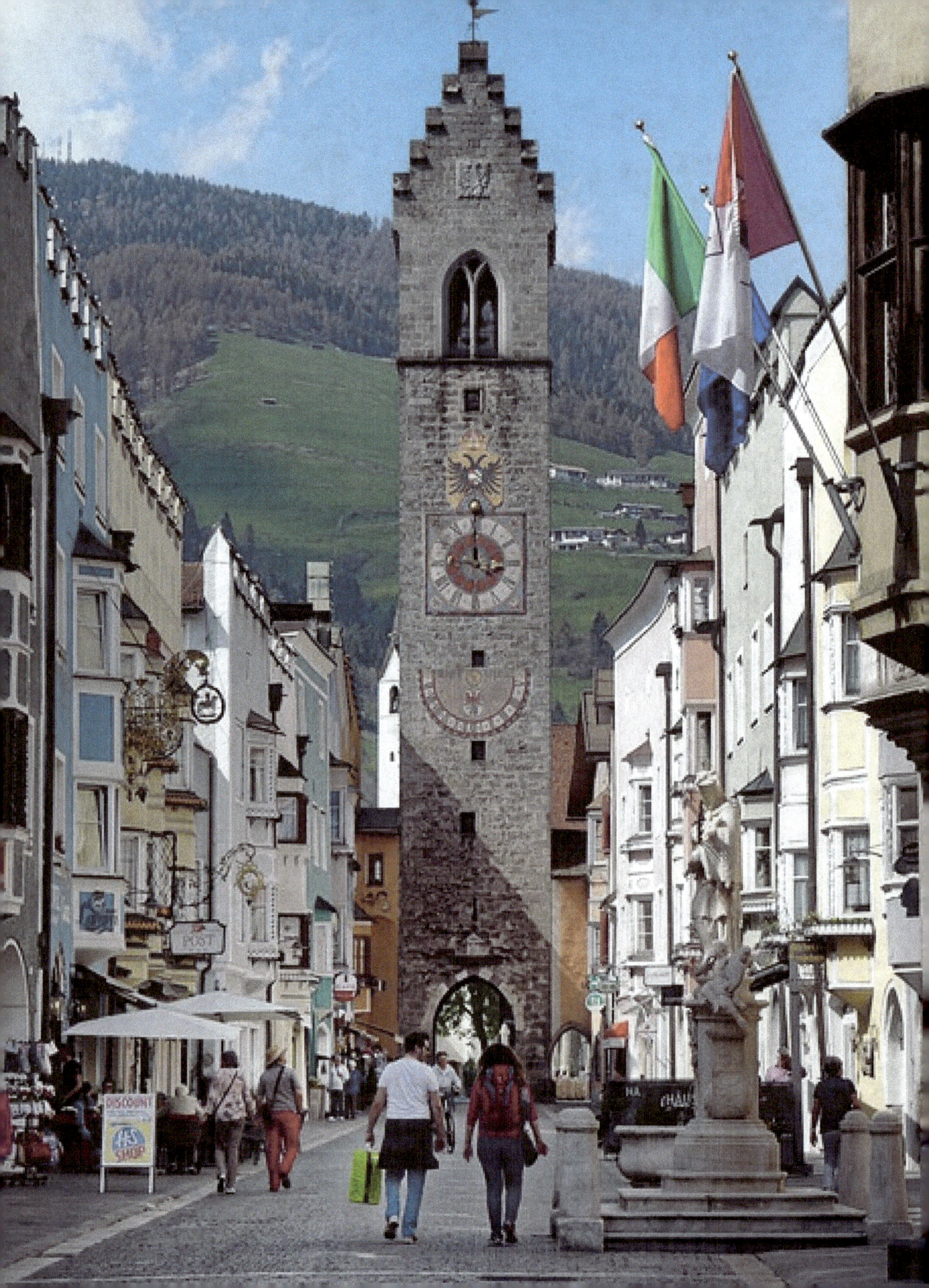
POST
DISCOUNT

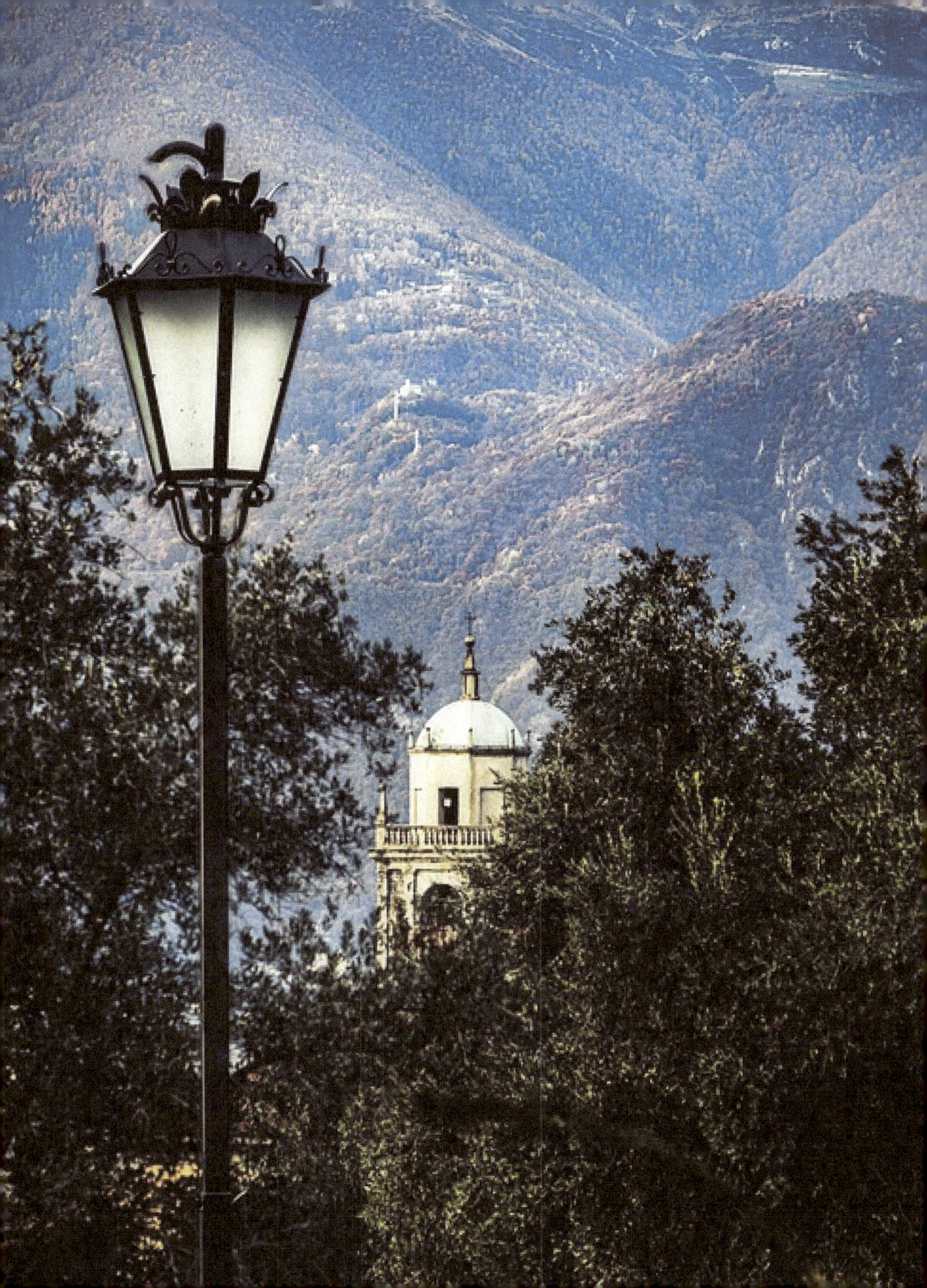

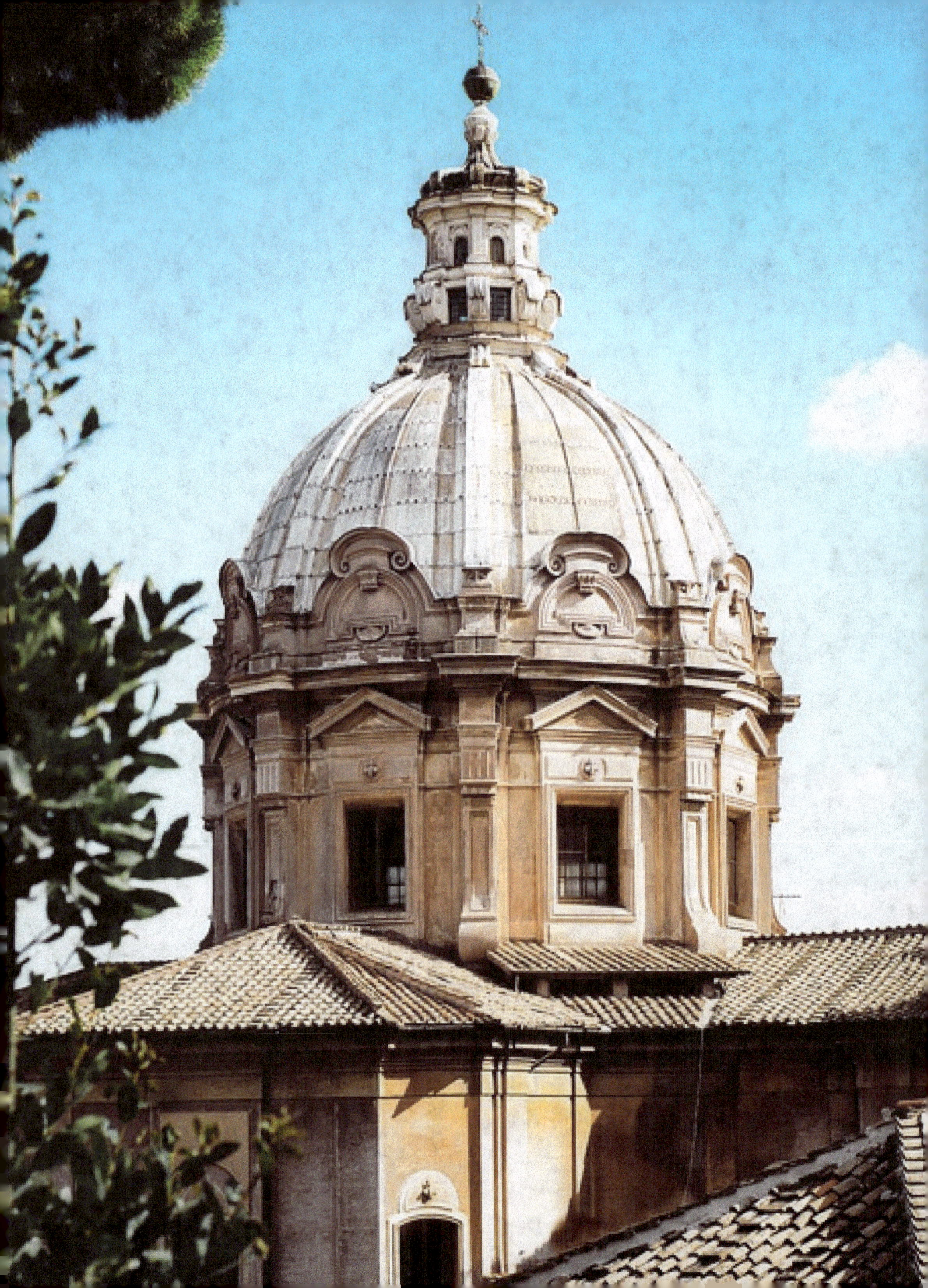

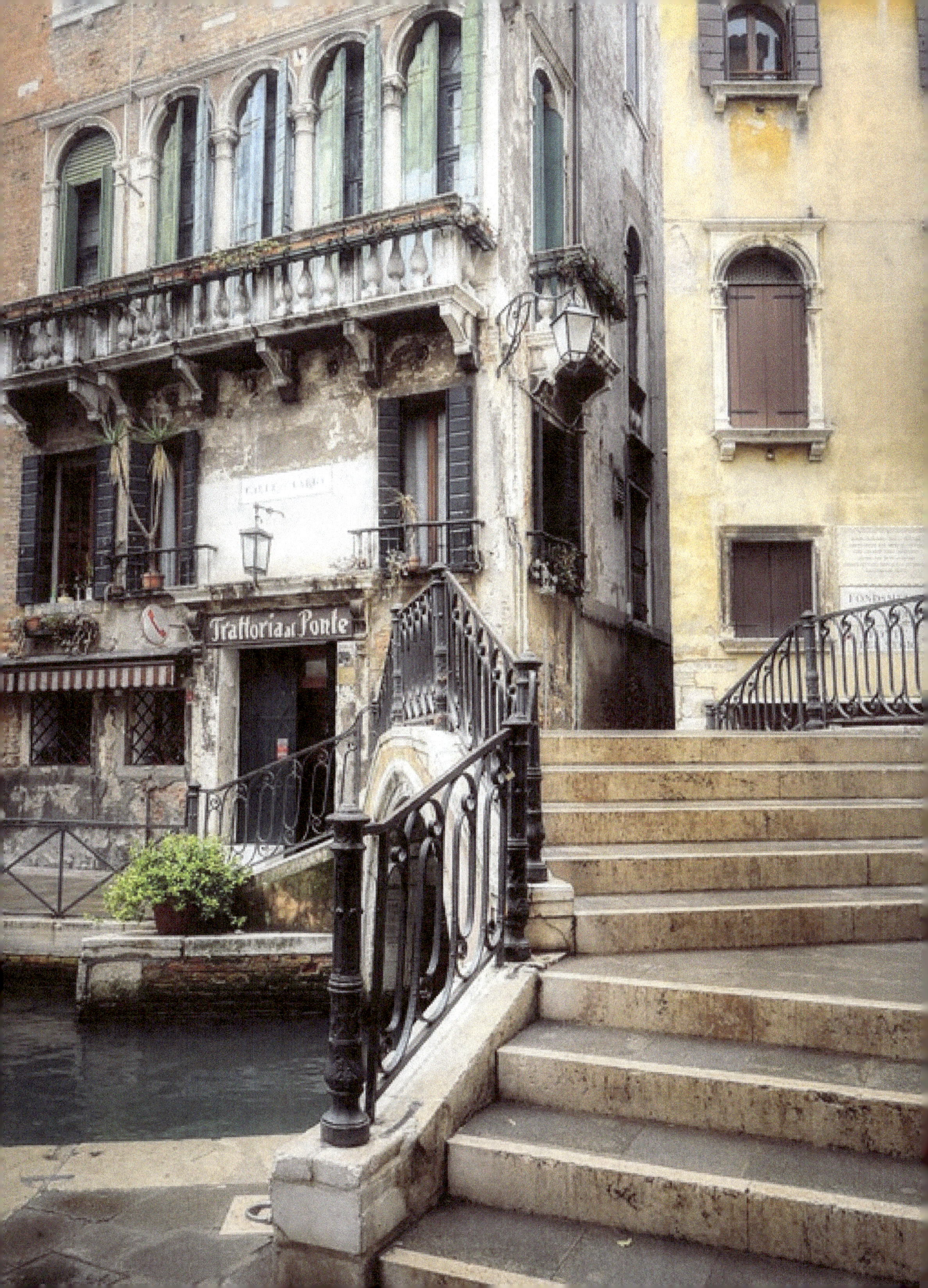
Trattoria al Ponte

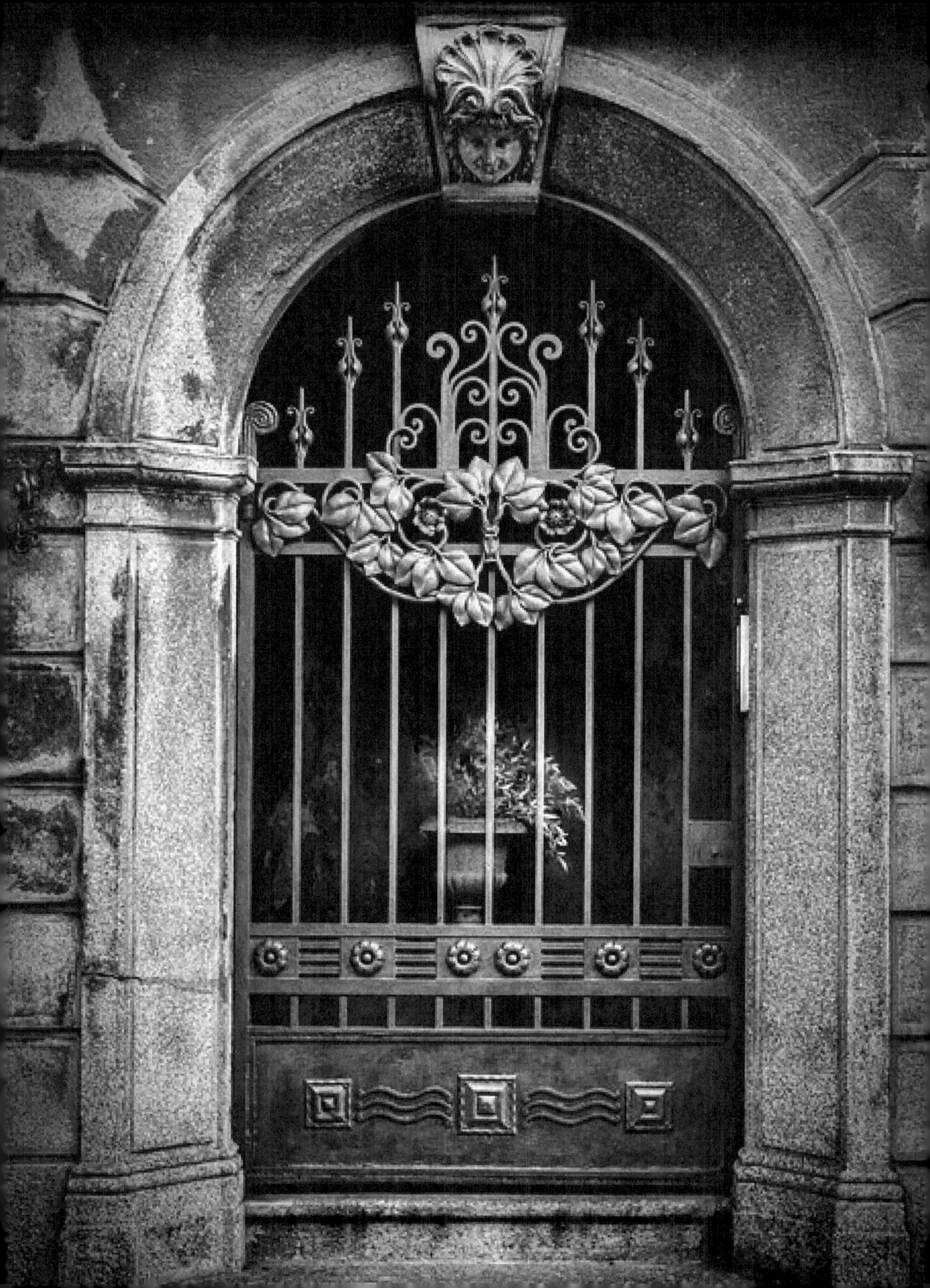

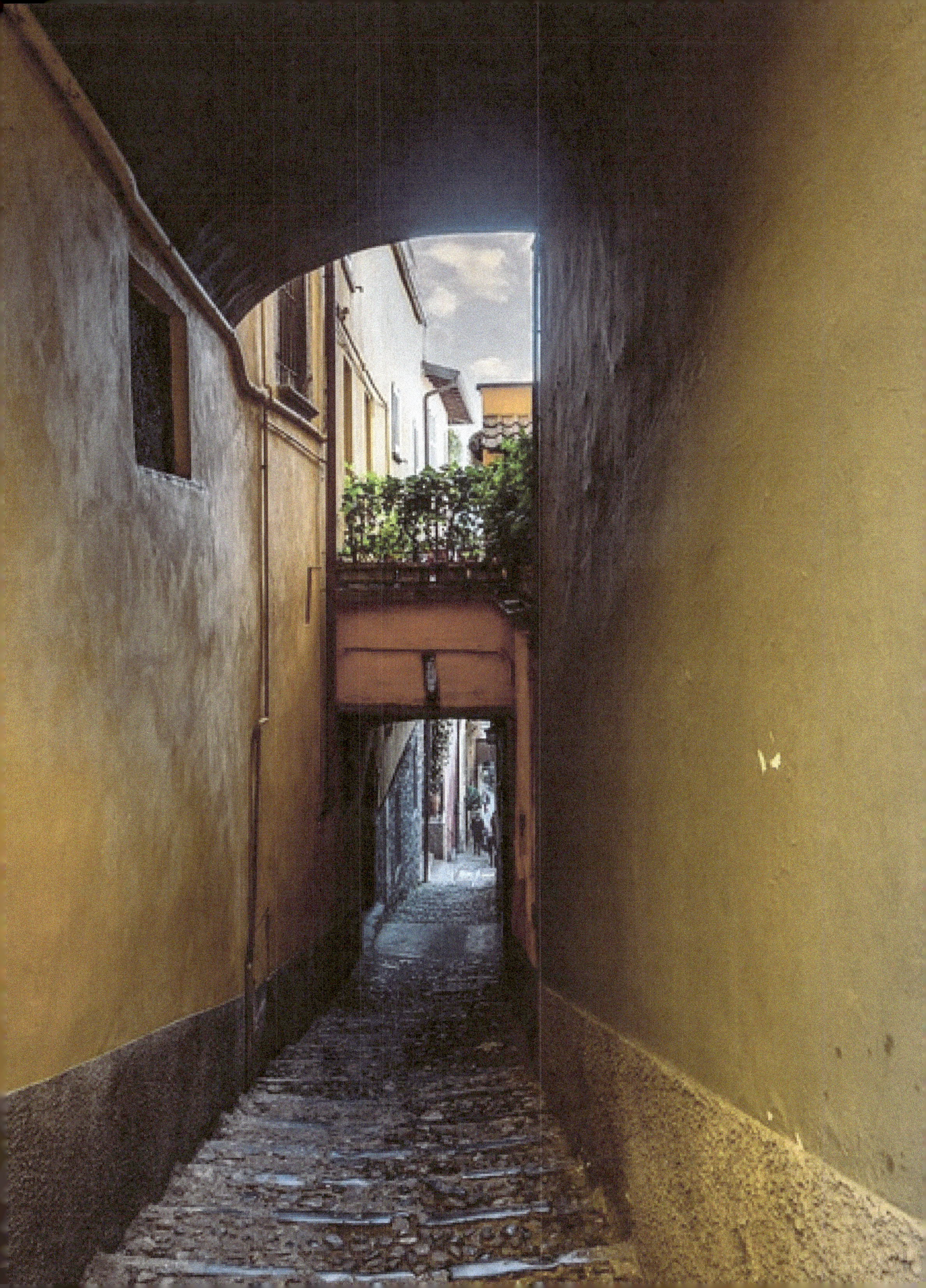

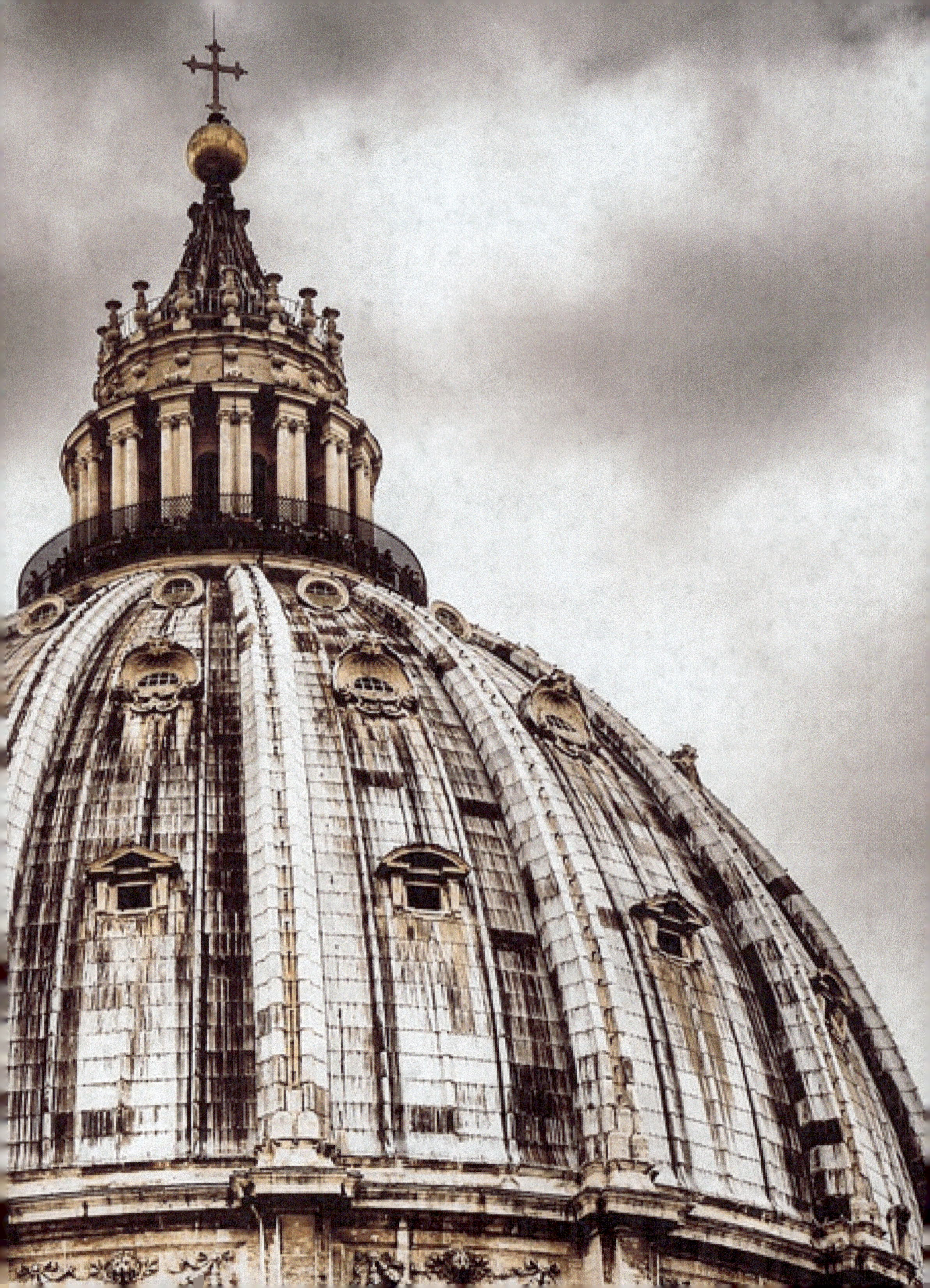

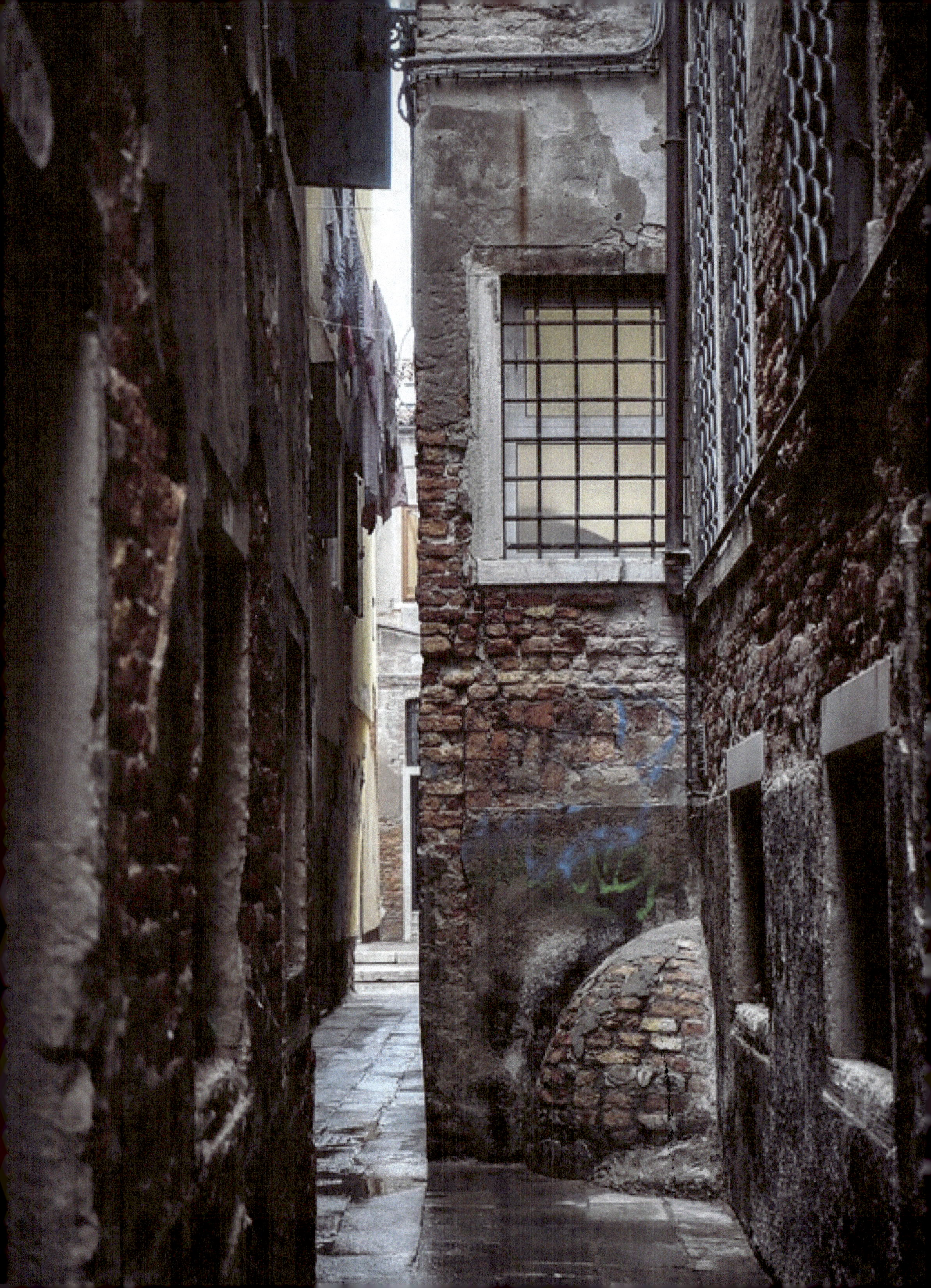

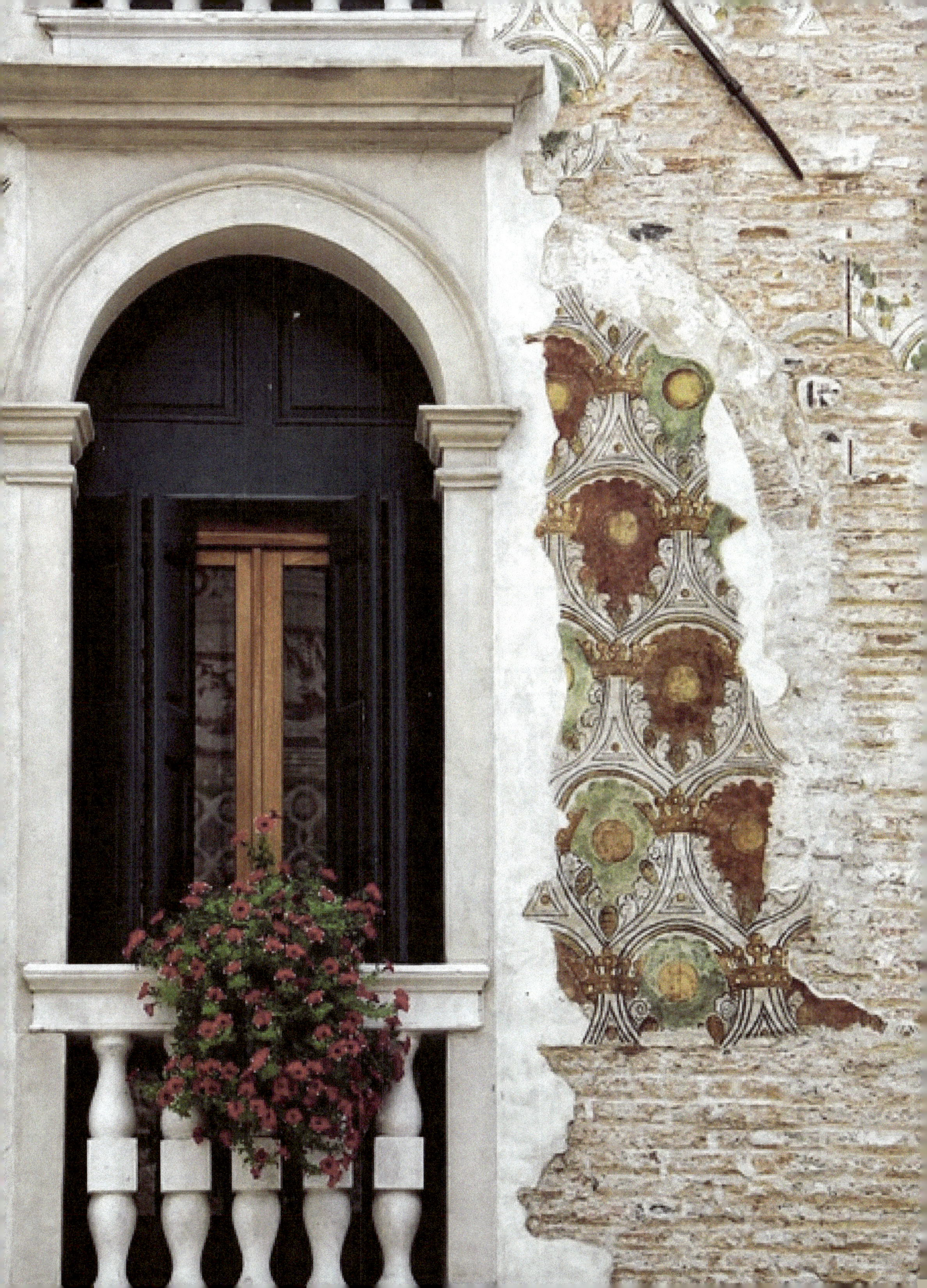

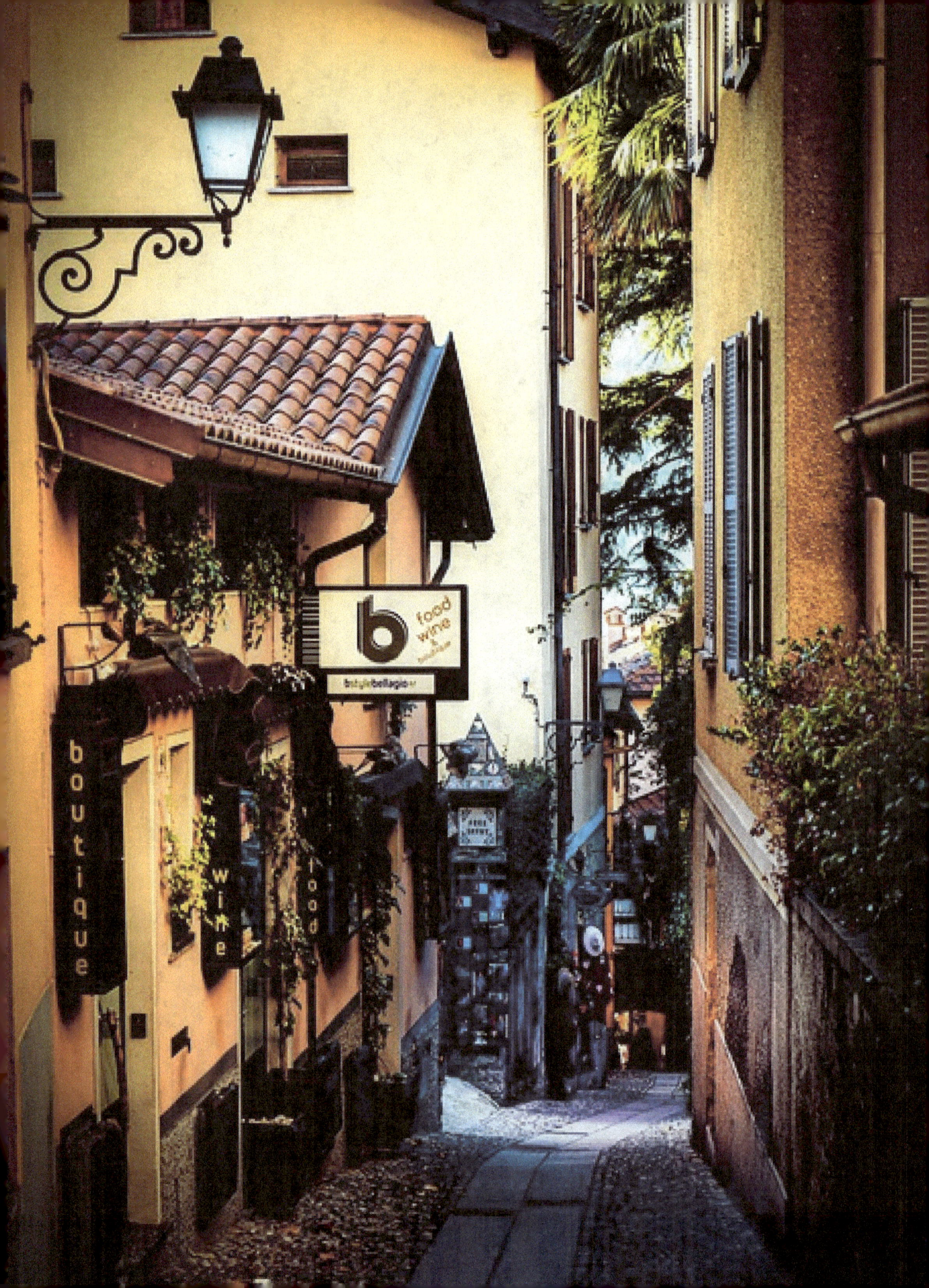
b
food
wine
&
boutique
wine
food

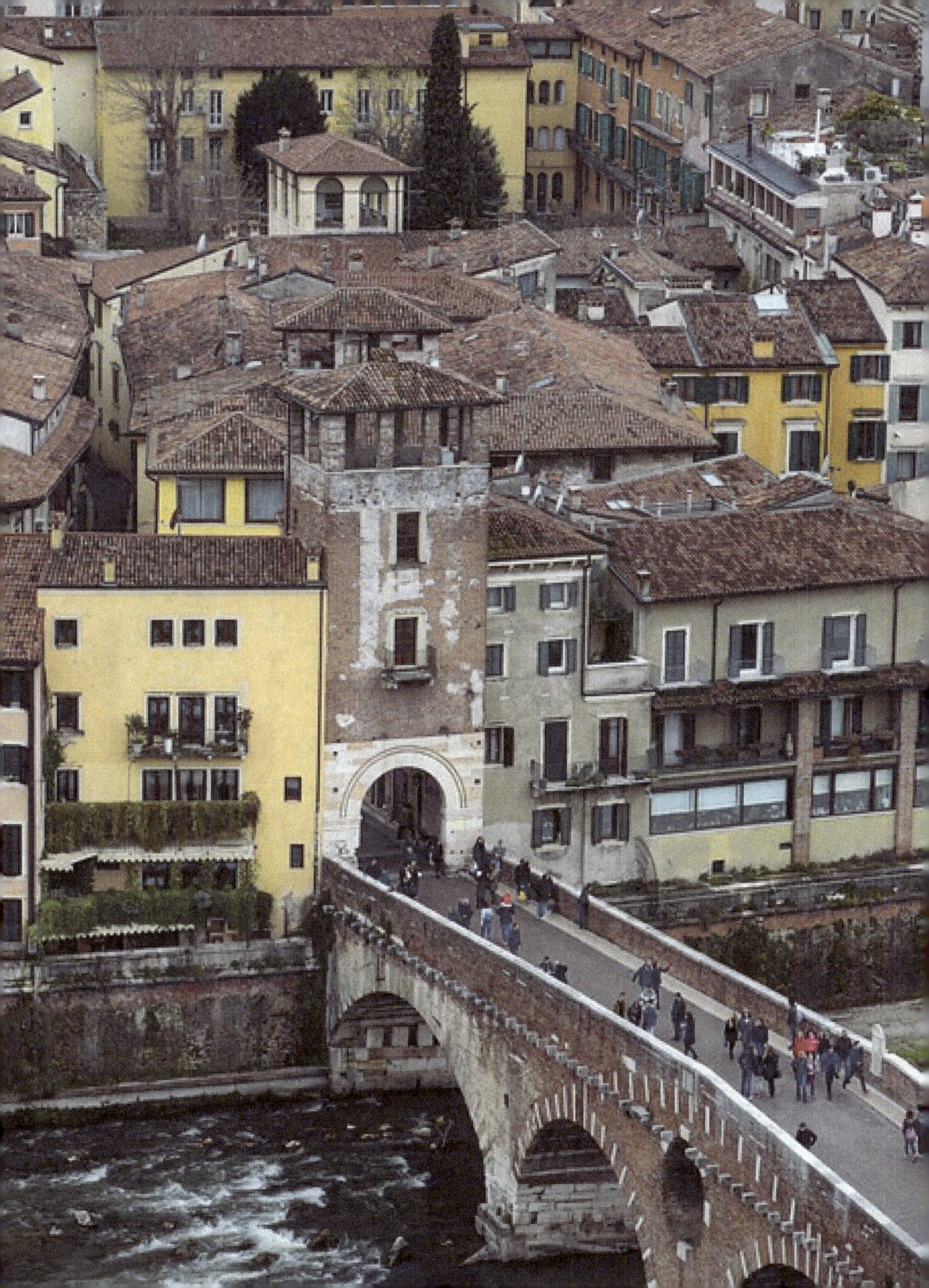

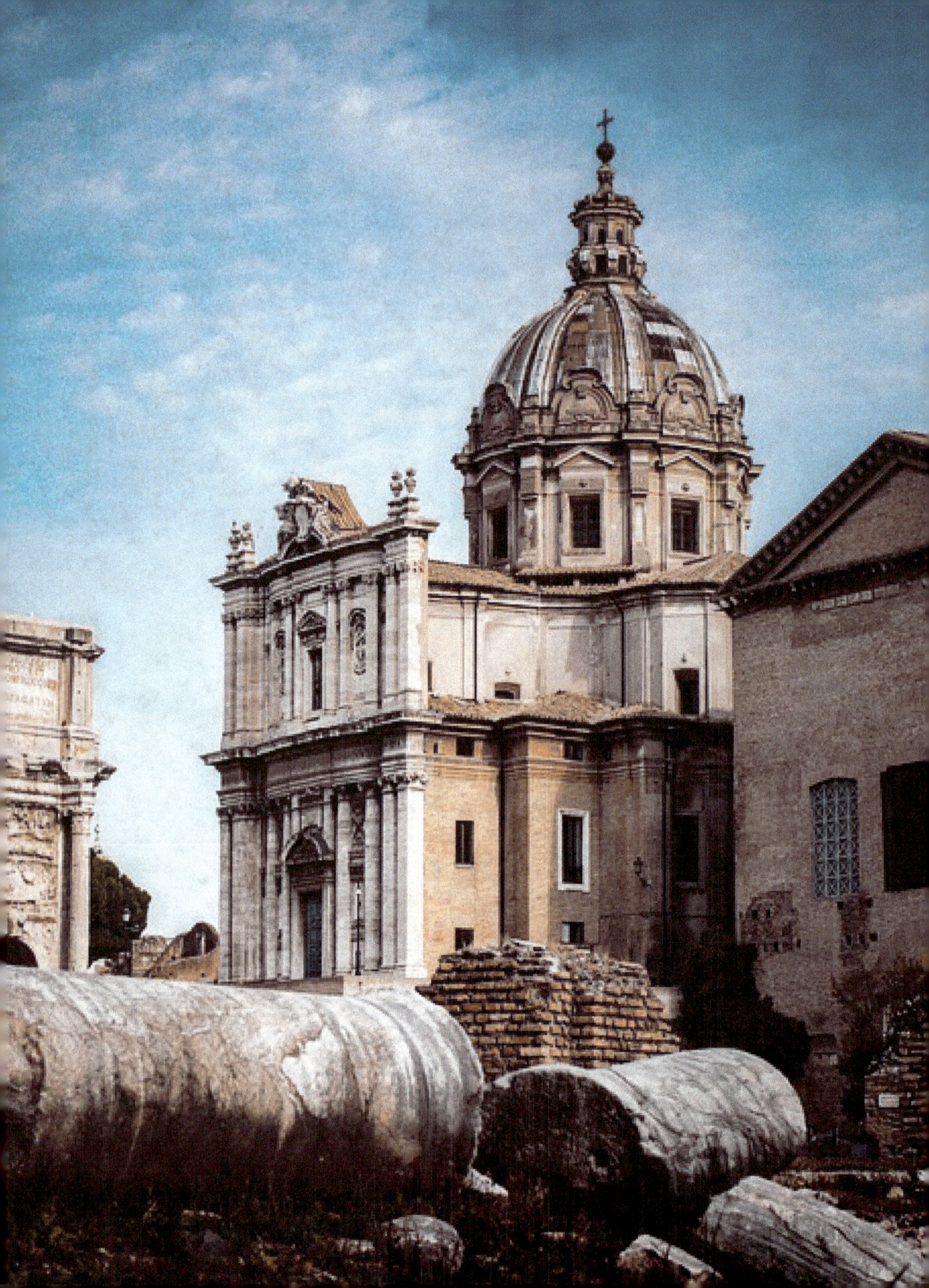

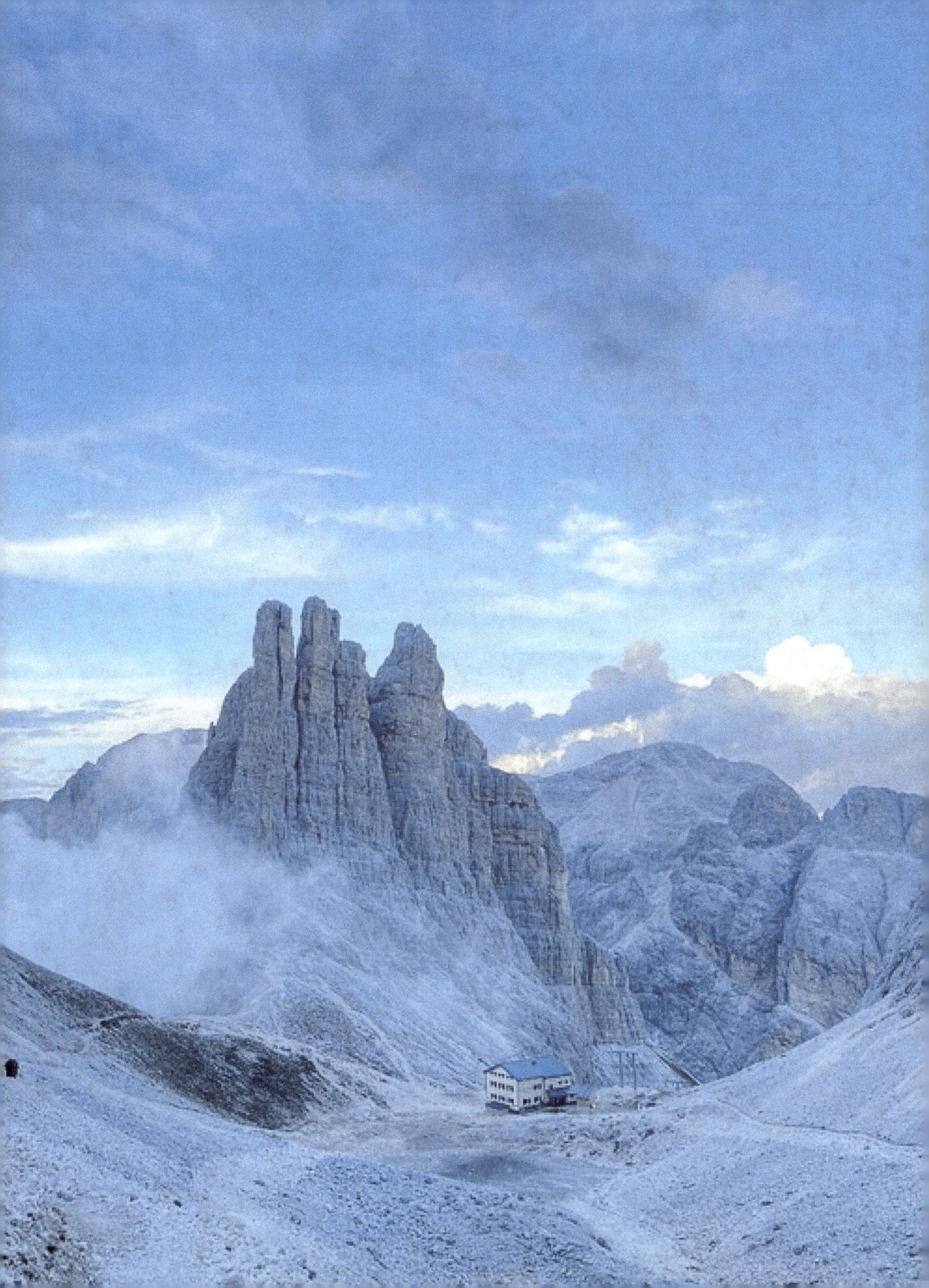

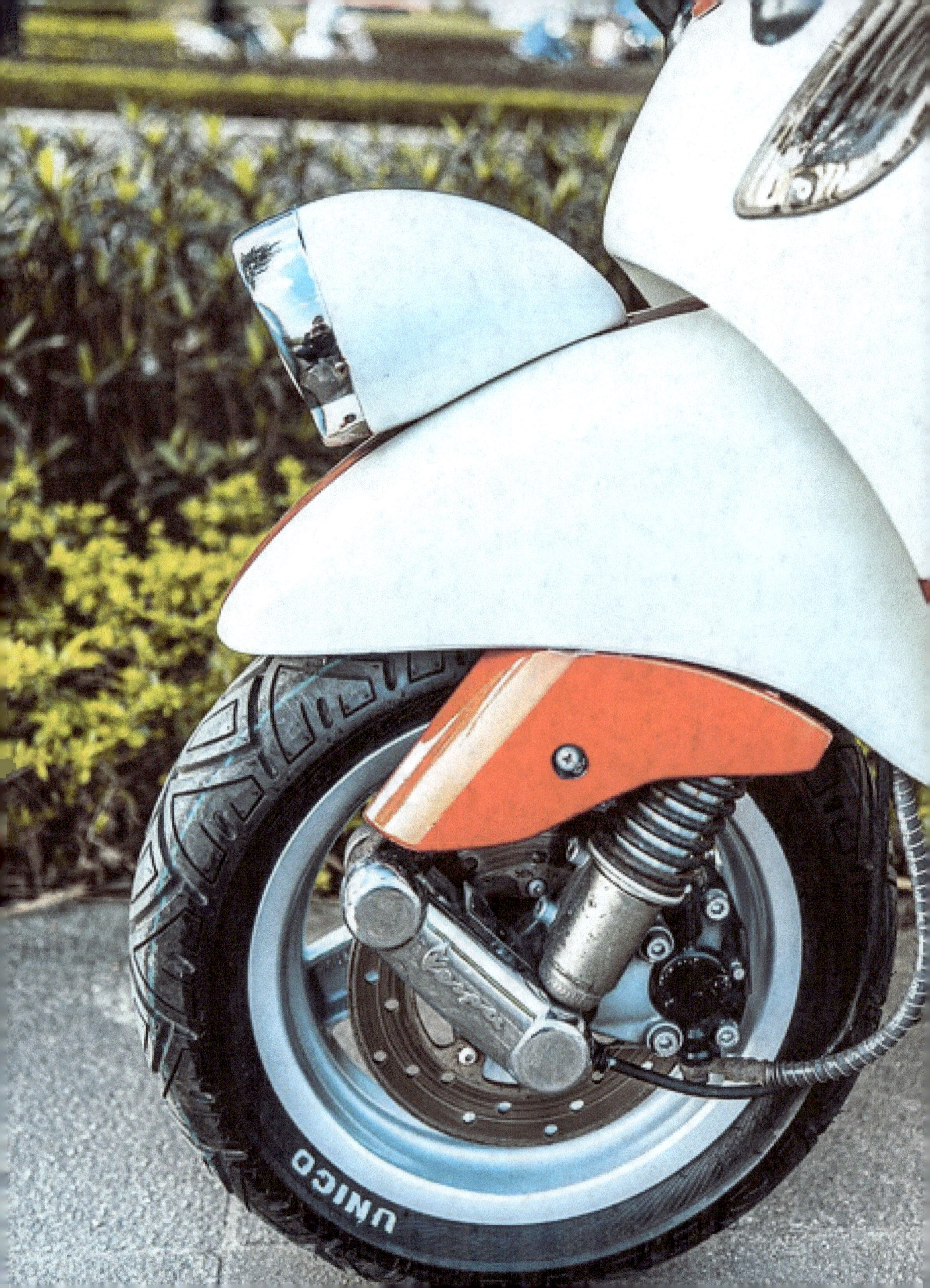
UNICO

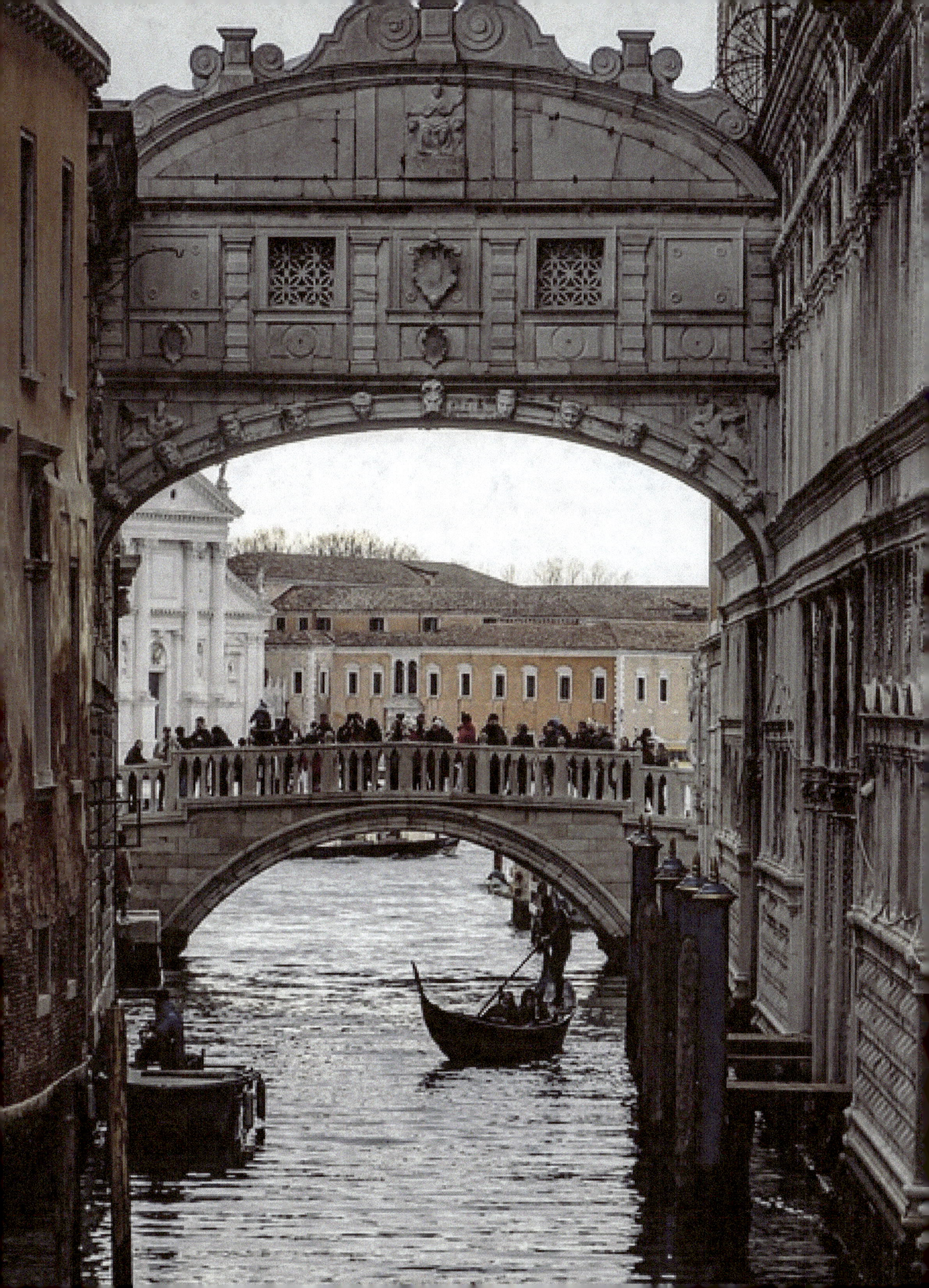

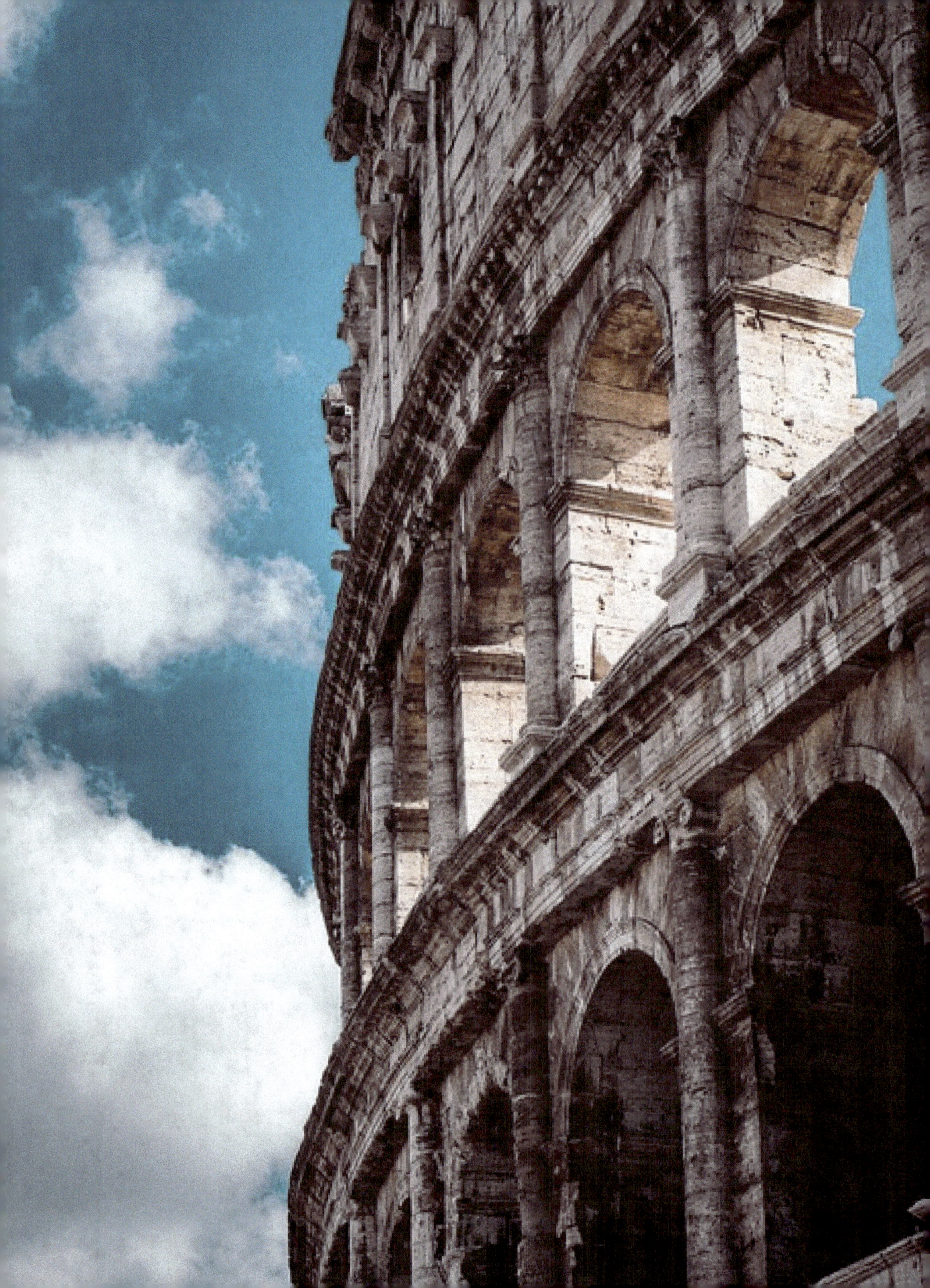

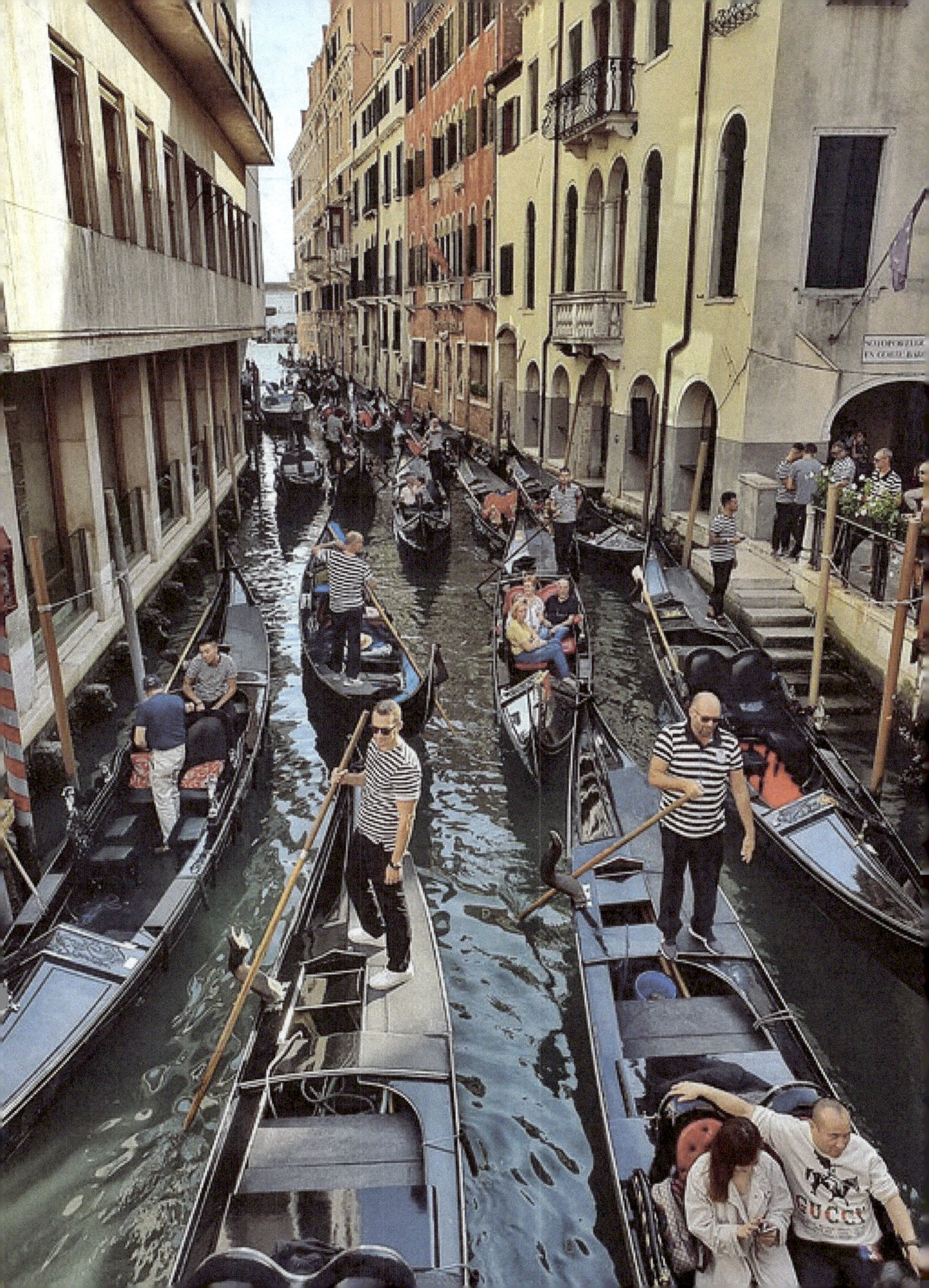
GUCCI

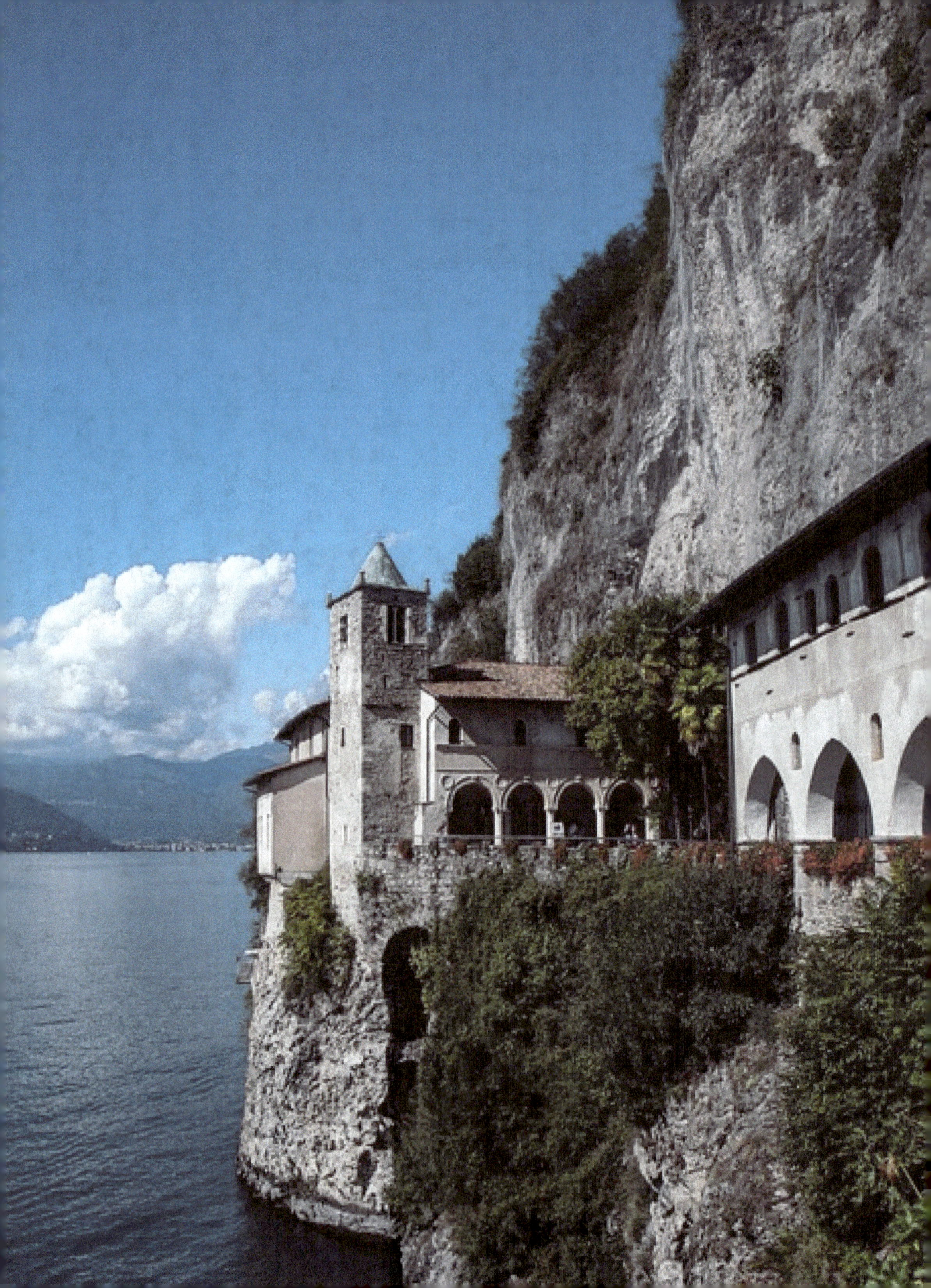

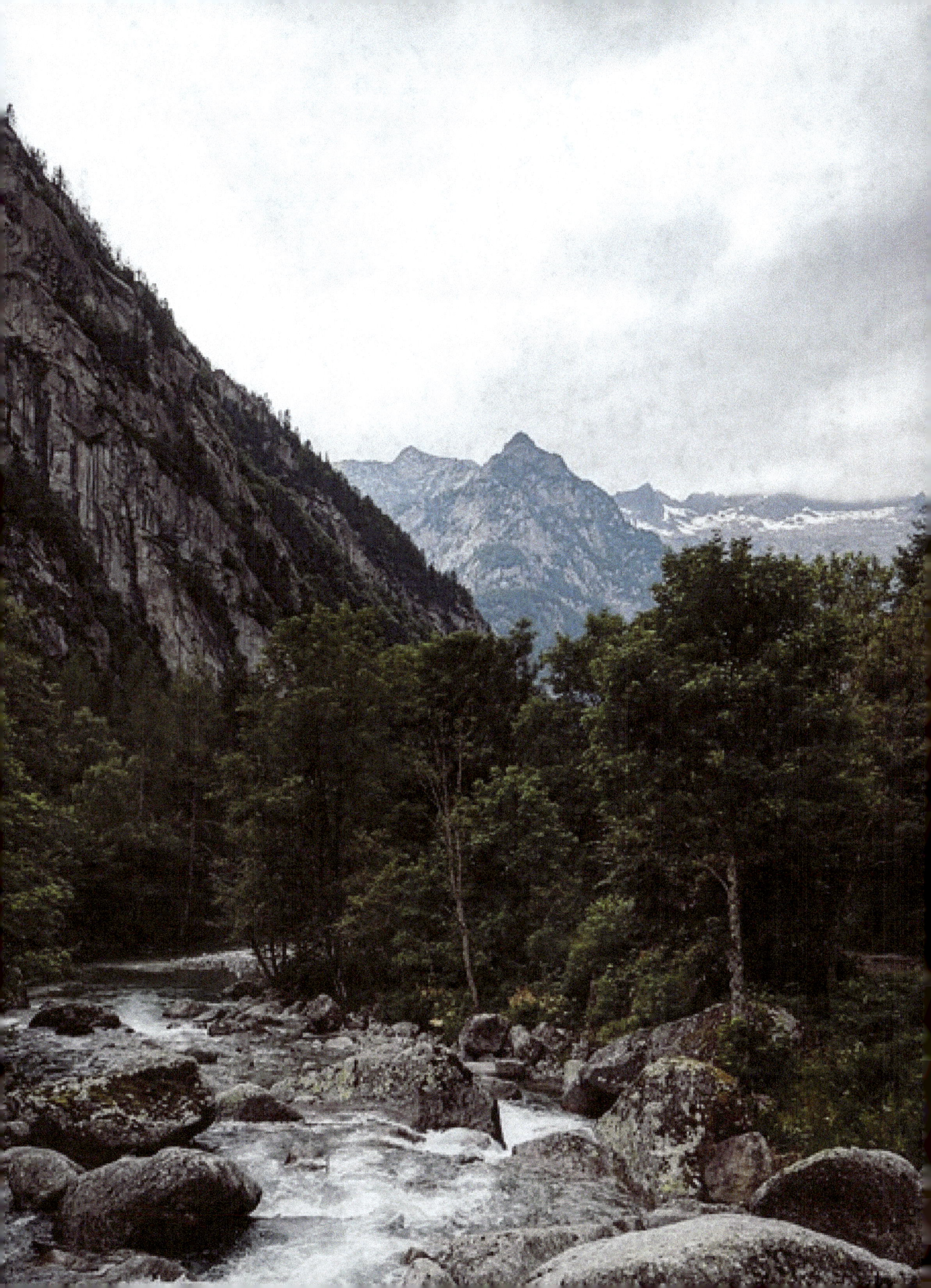

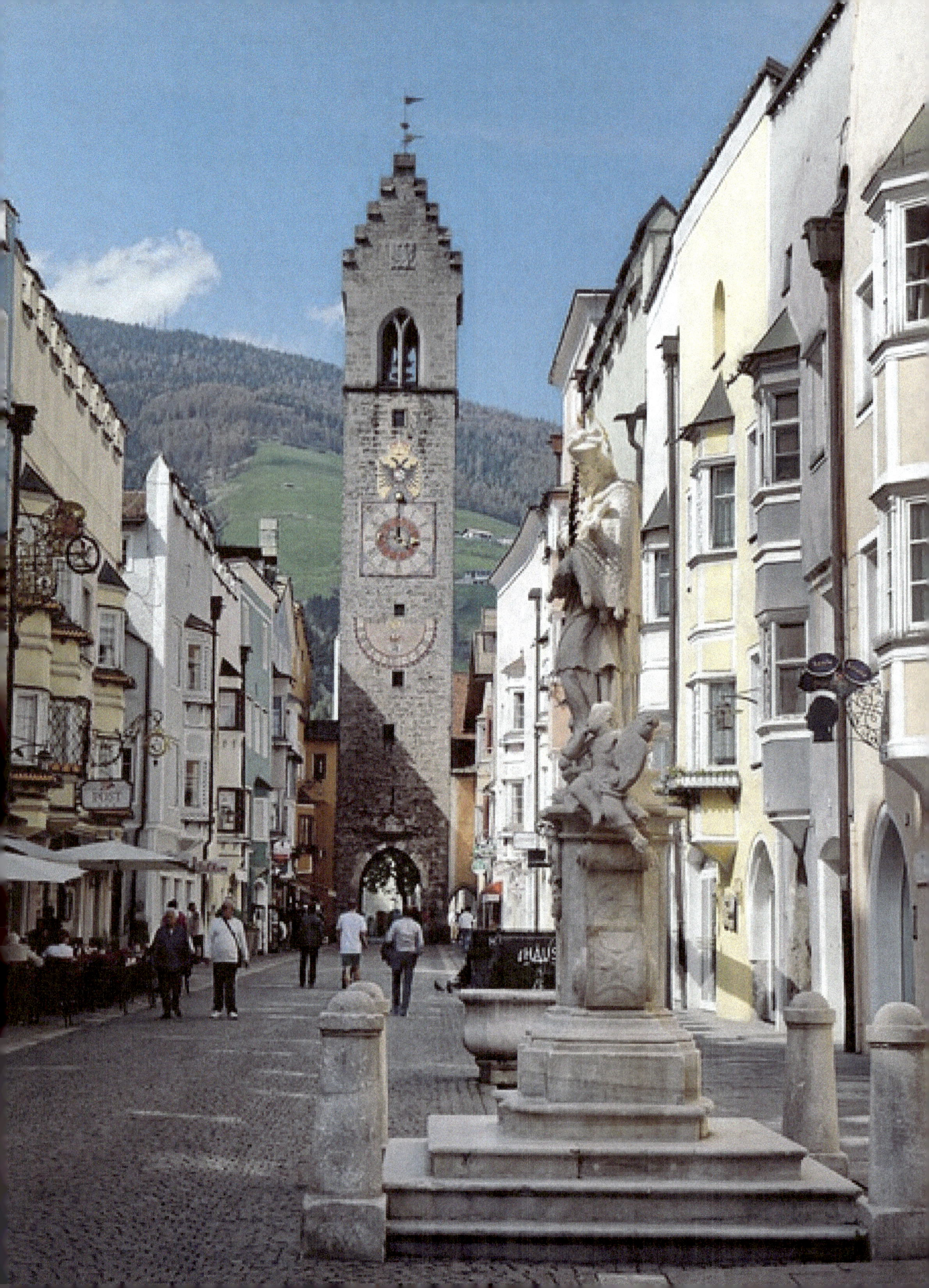
POST

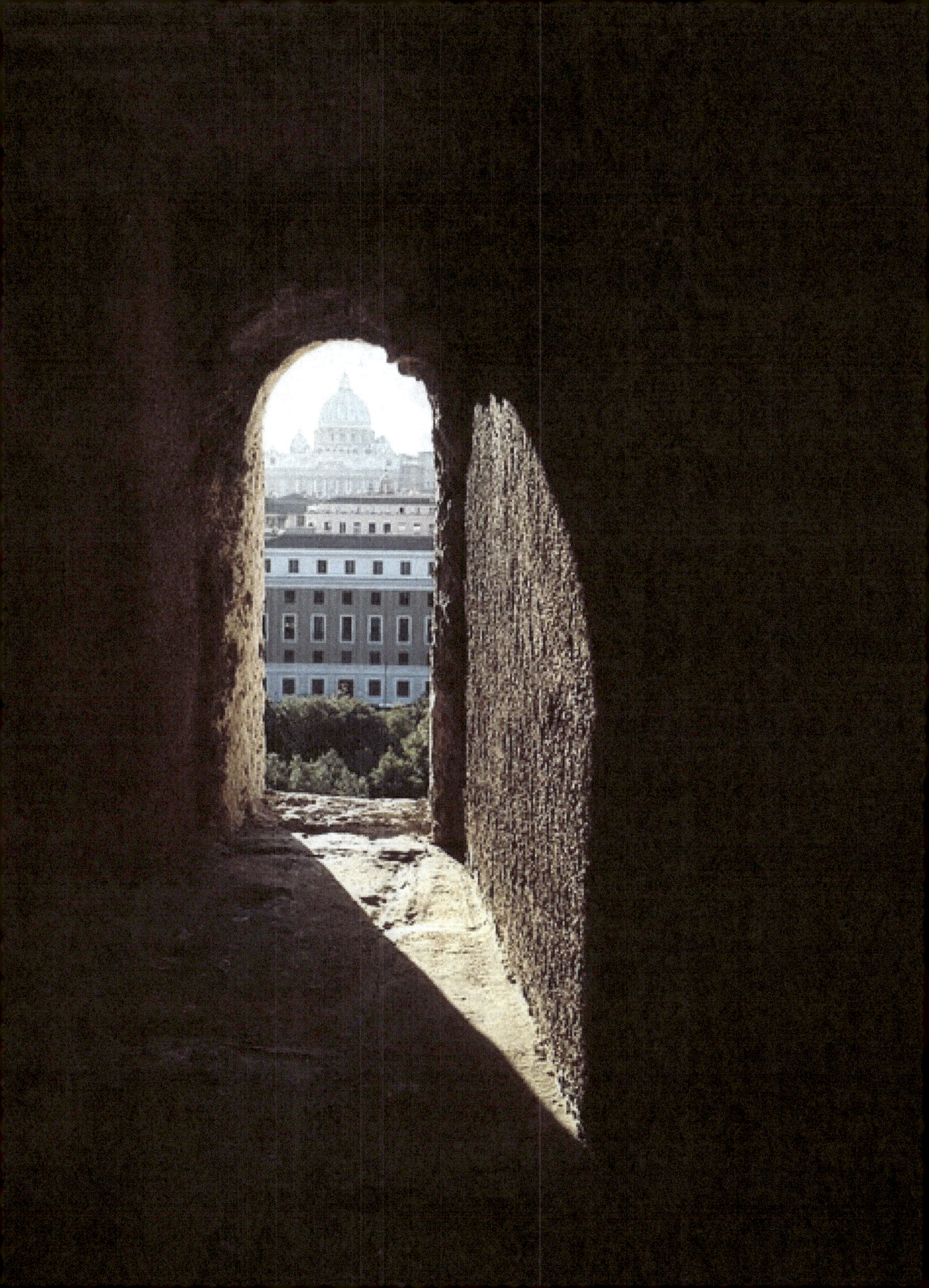

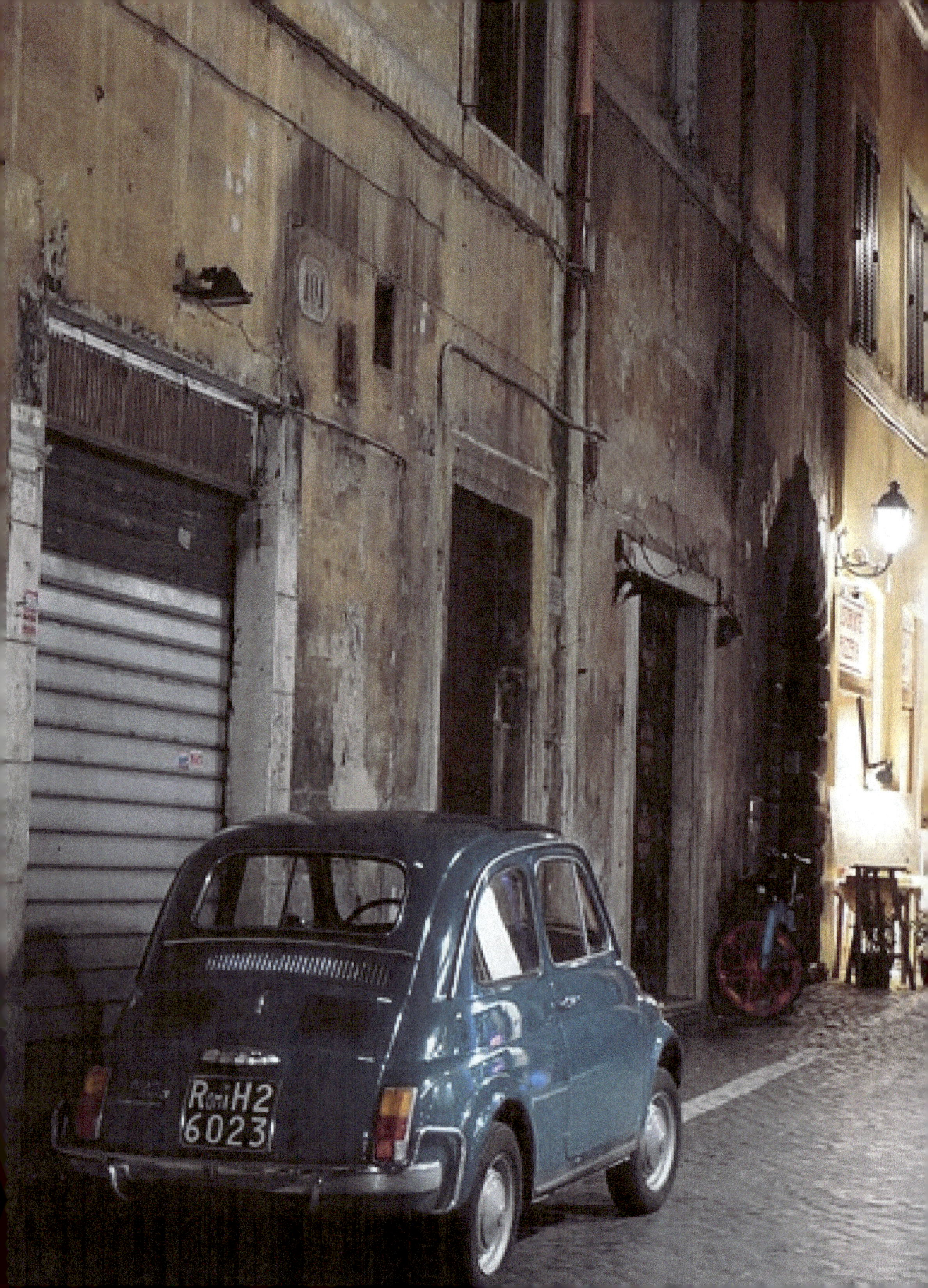
H2
6023

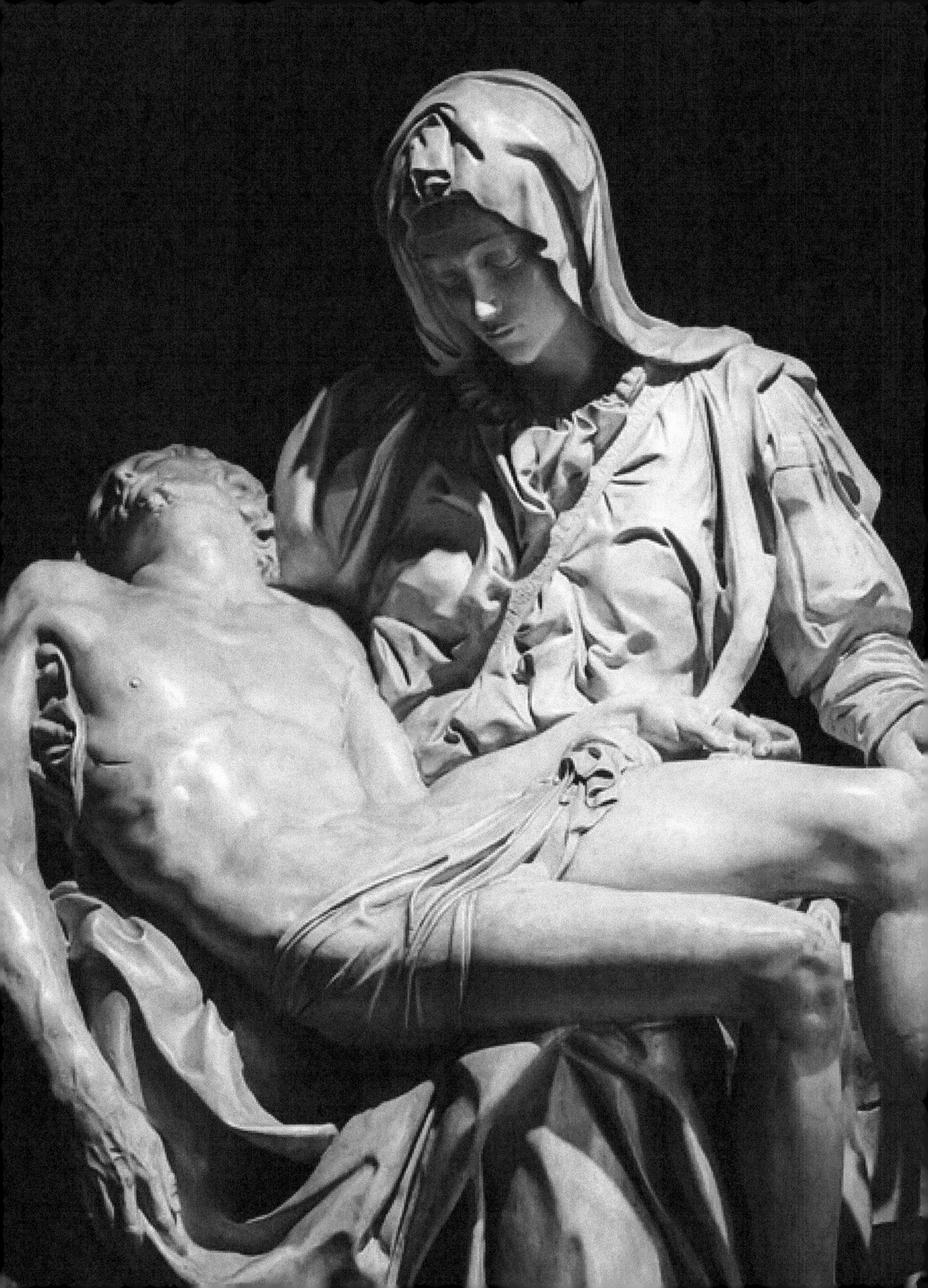

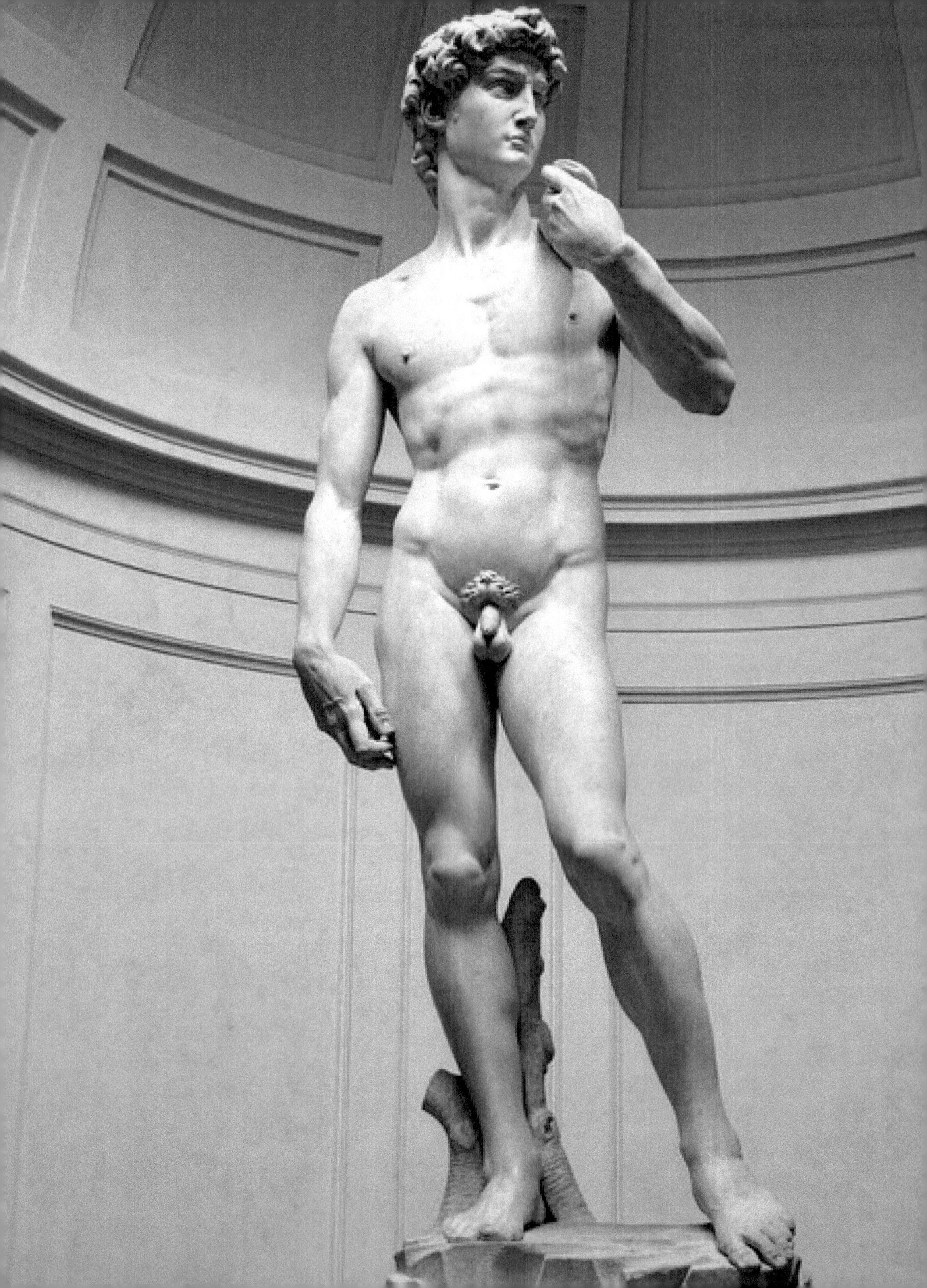

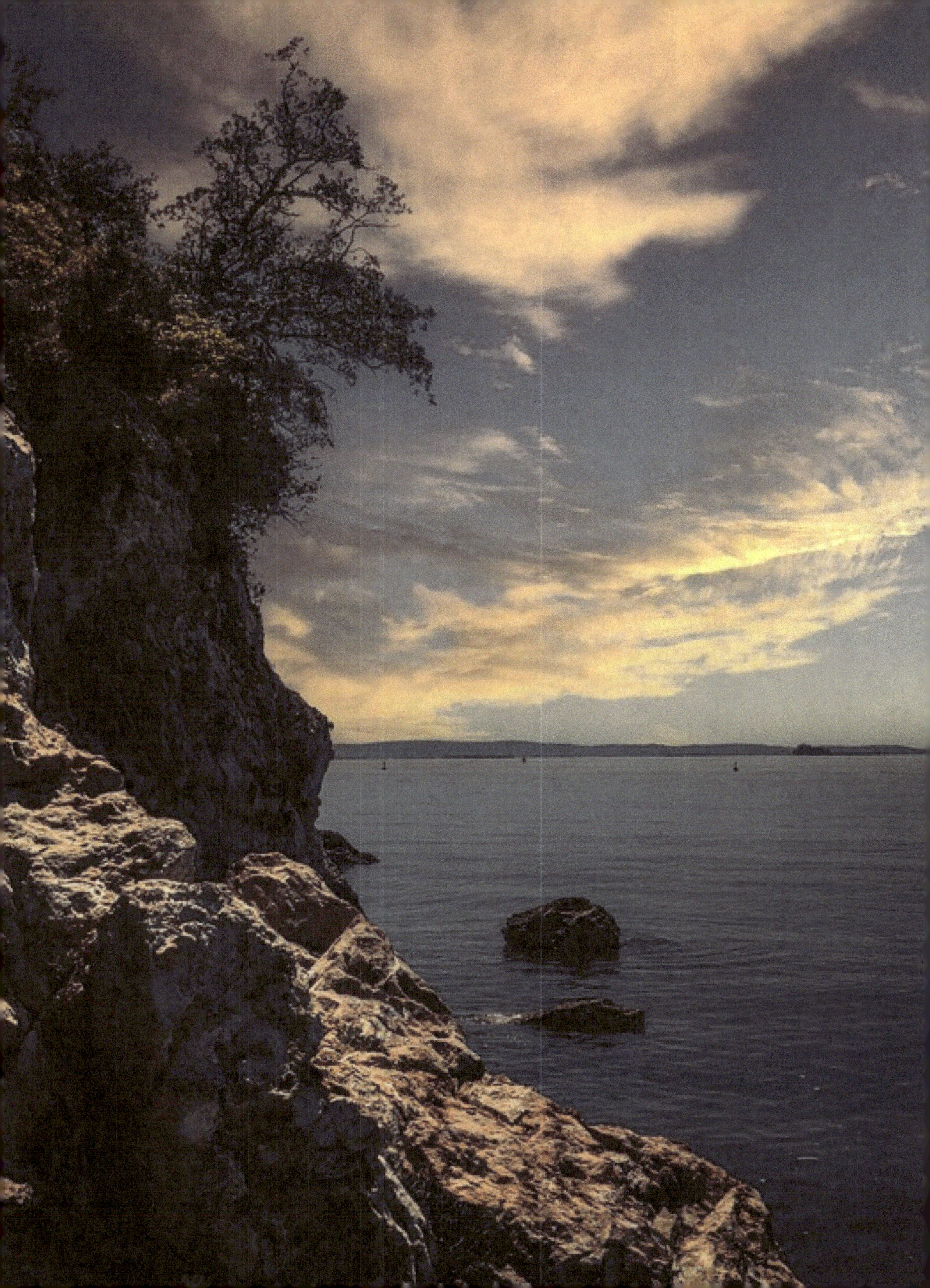

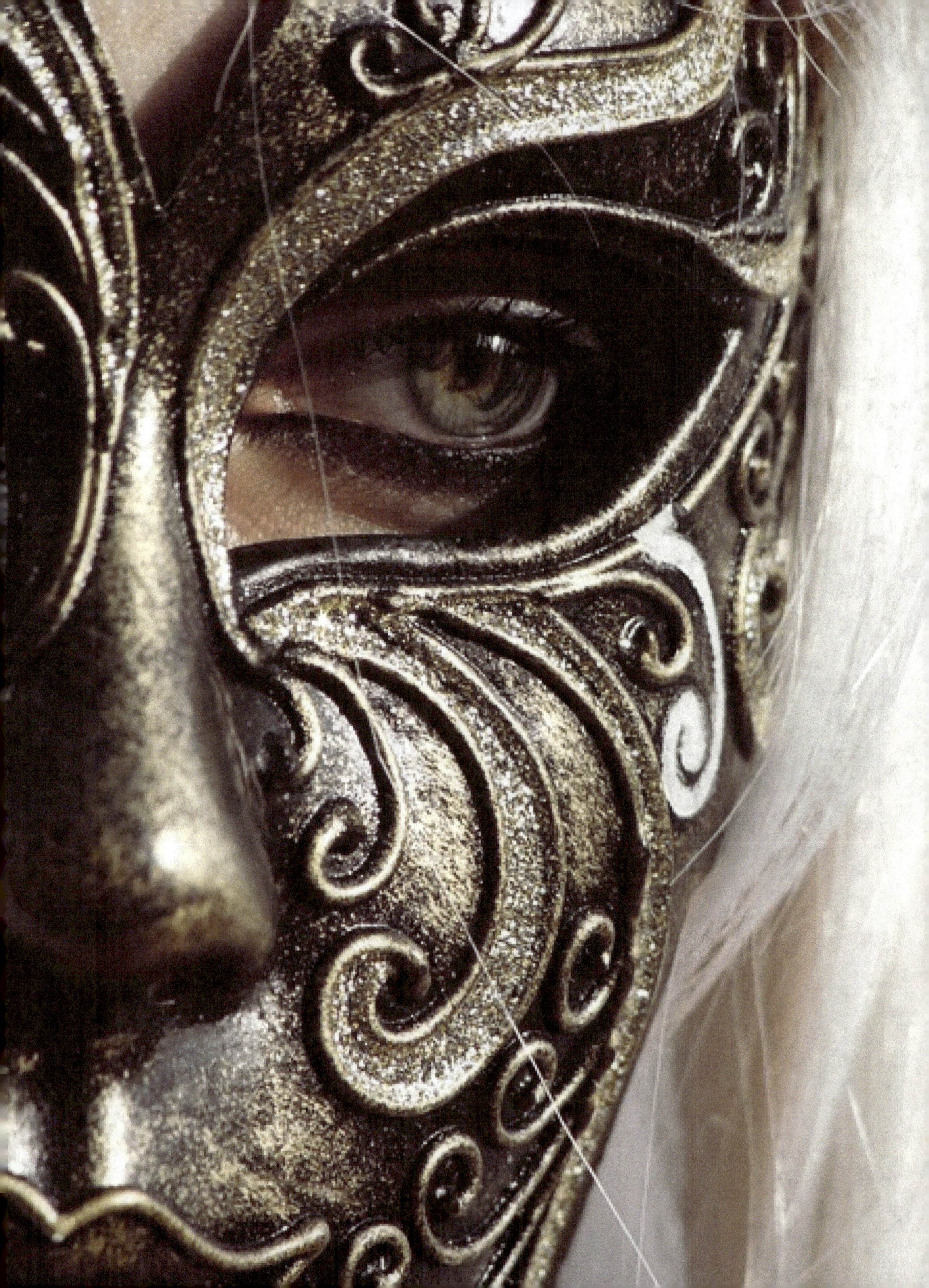

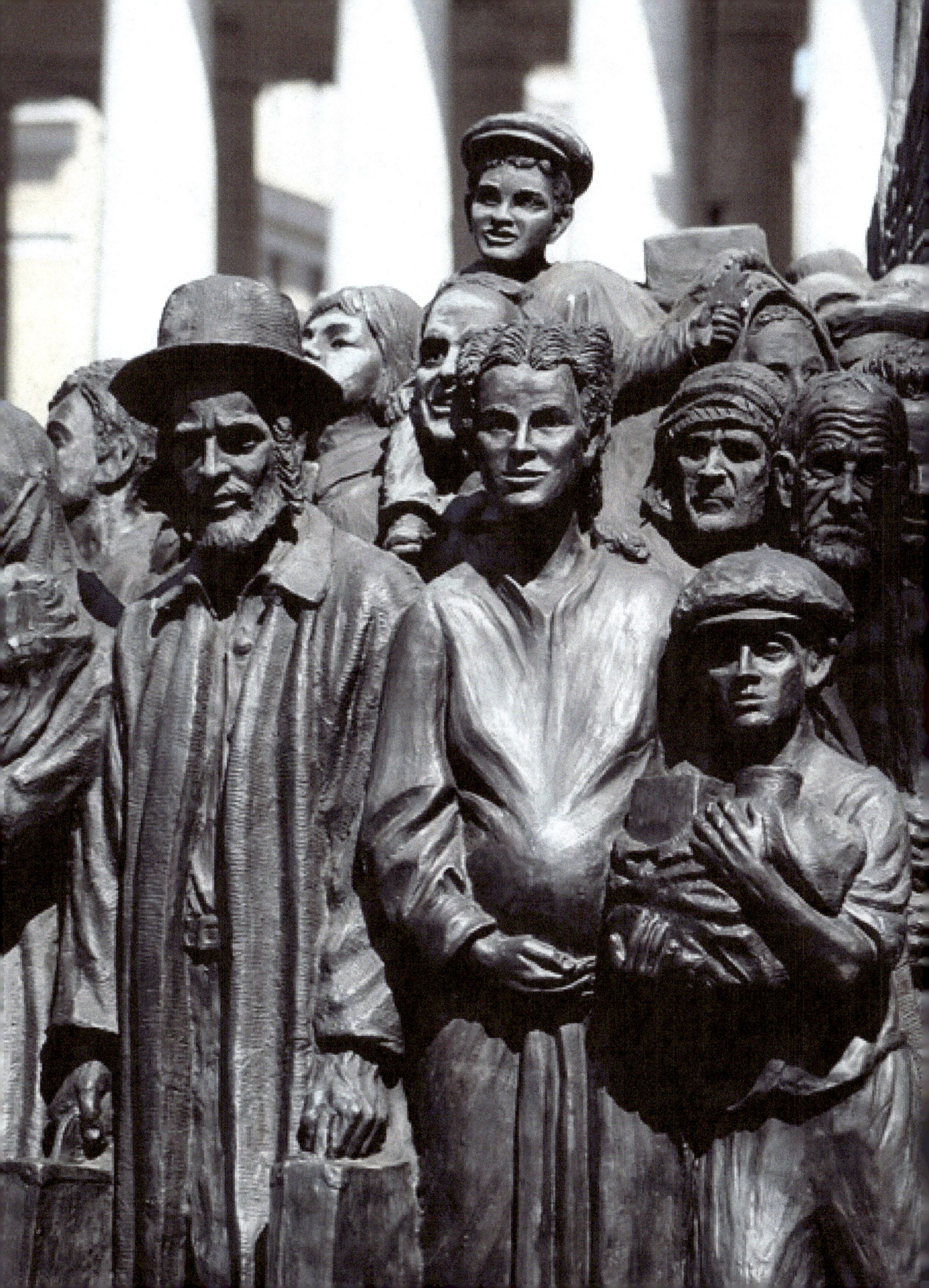

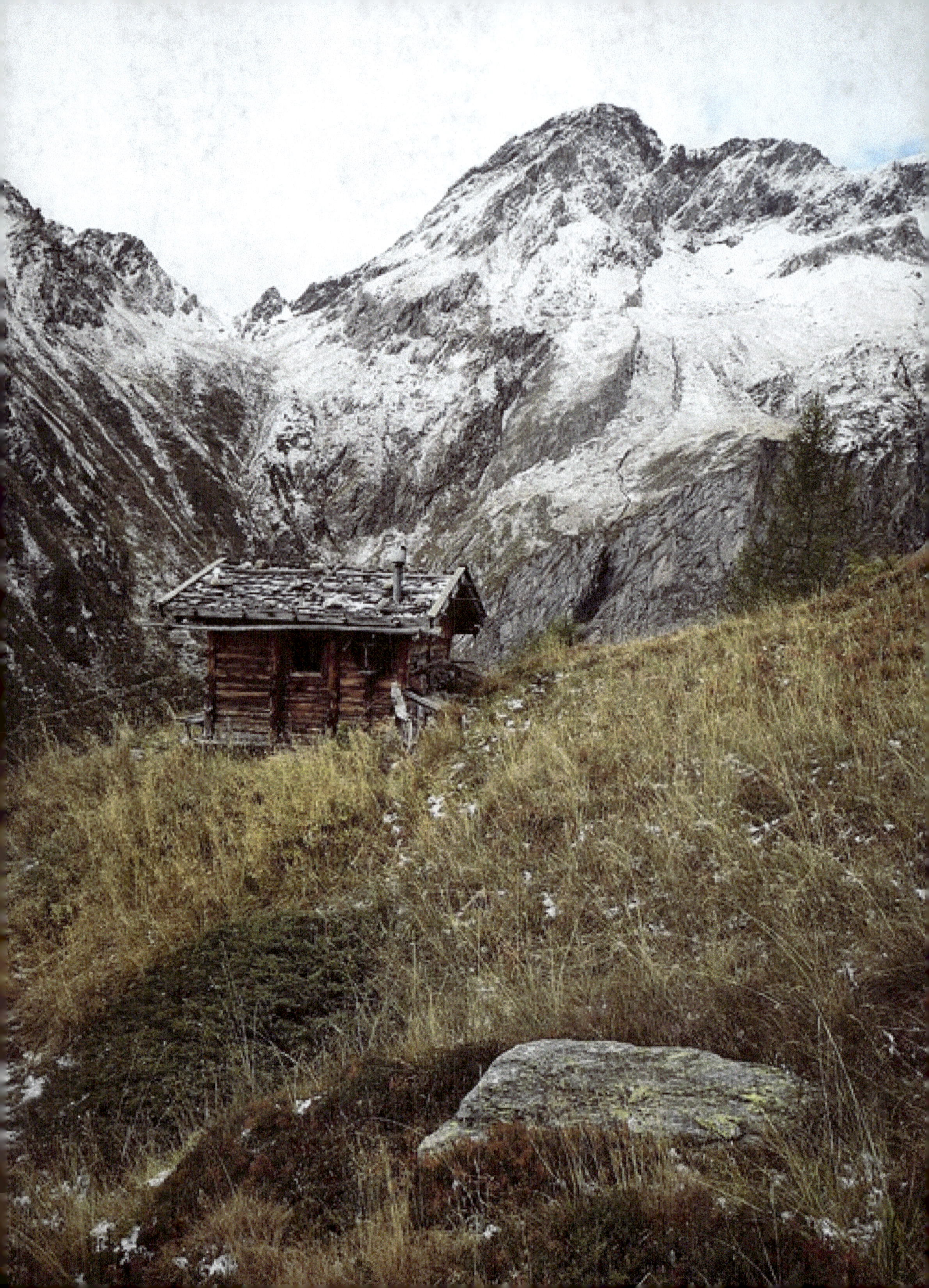

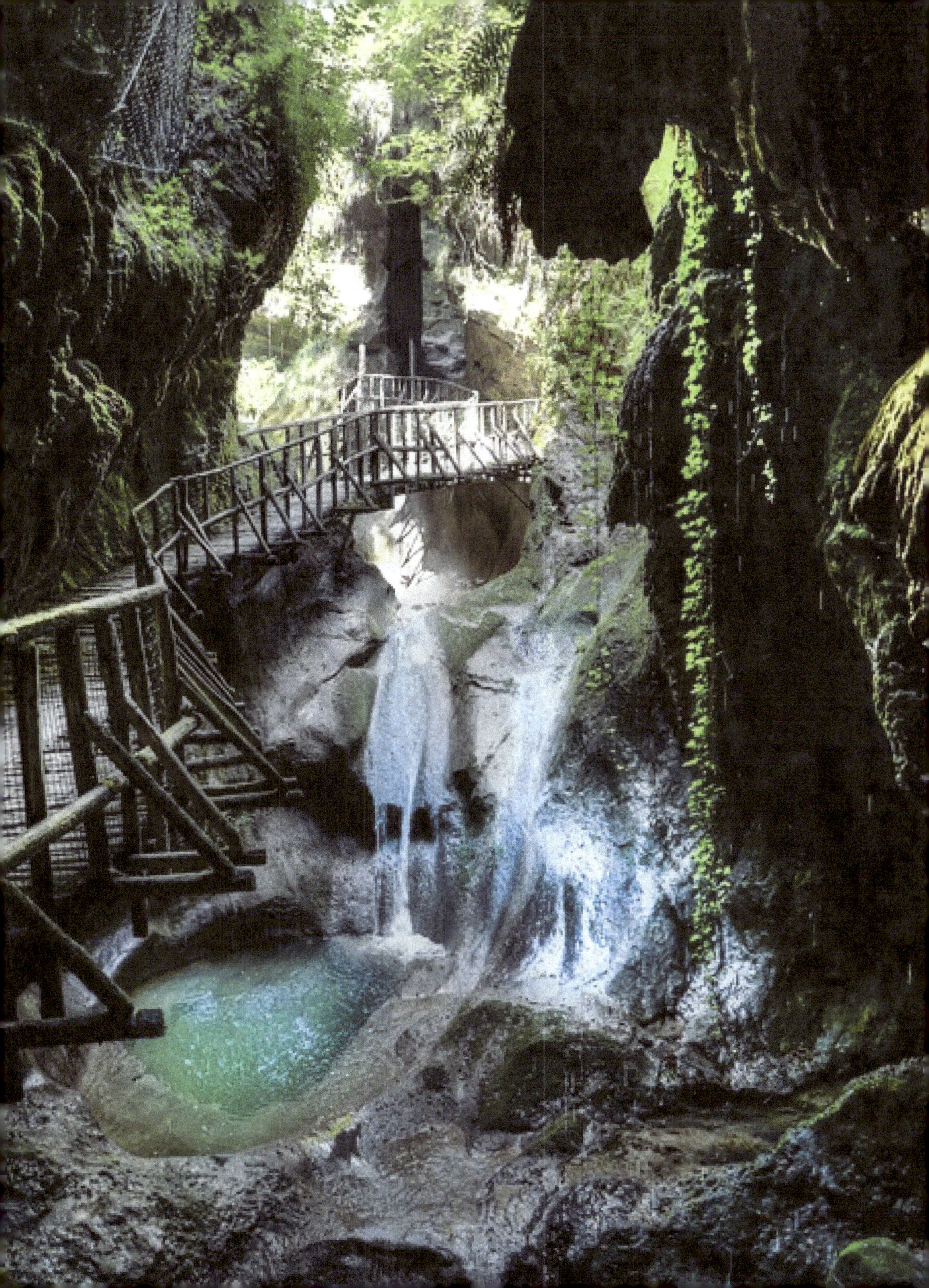

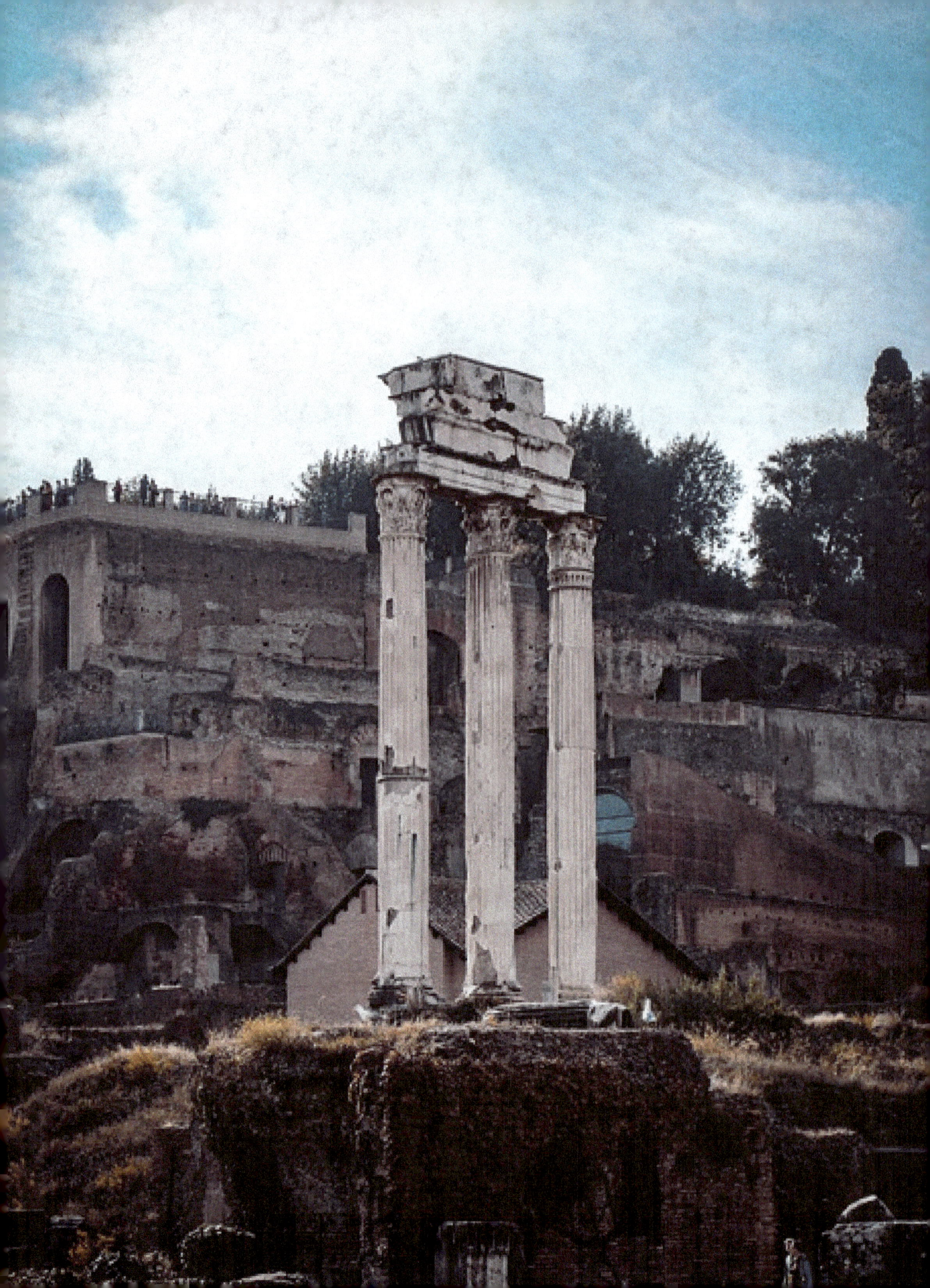

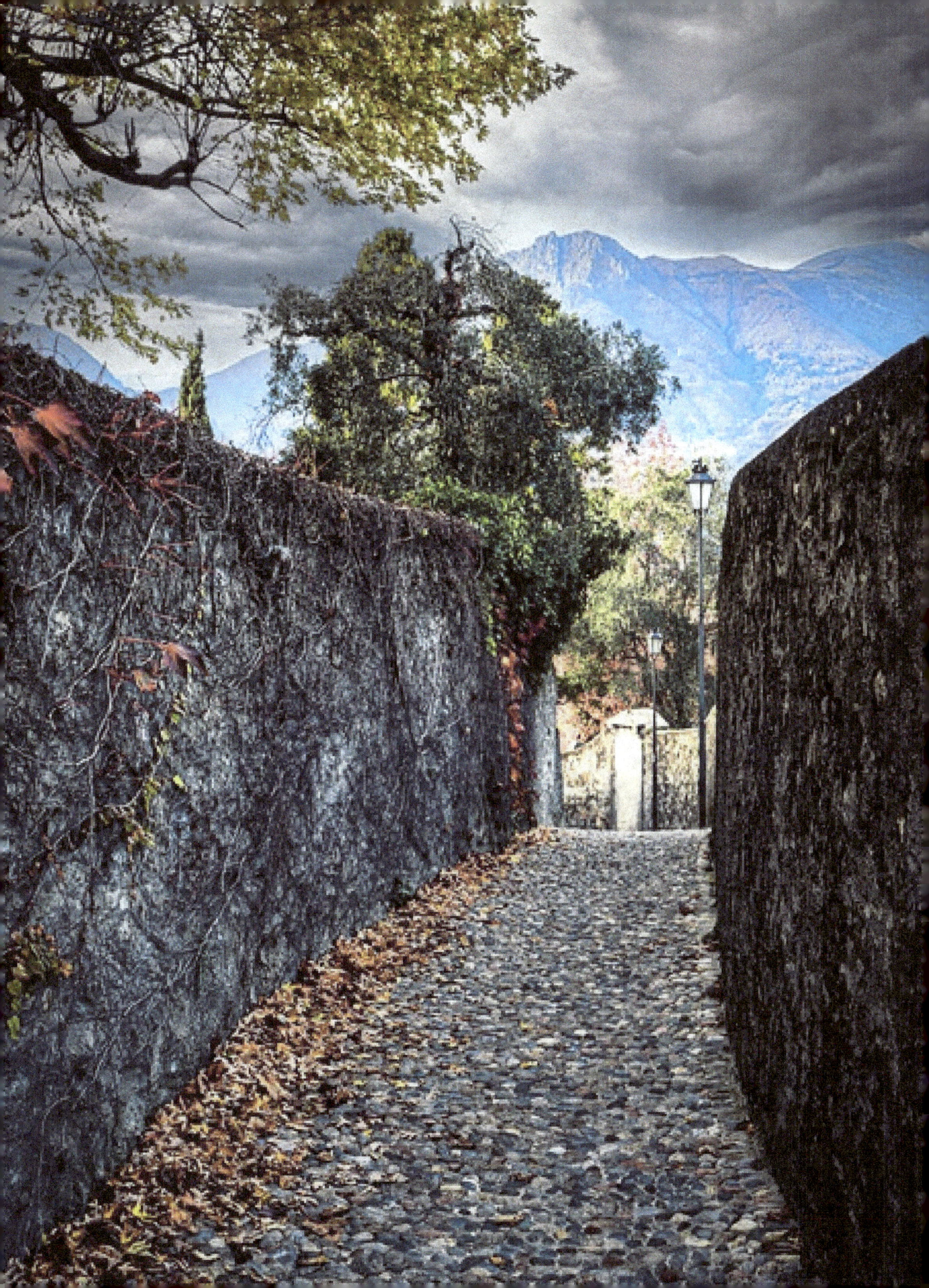

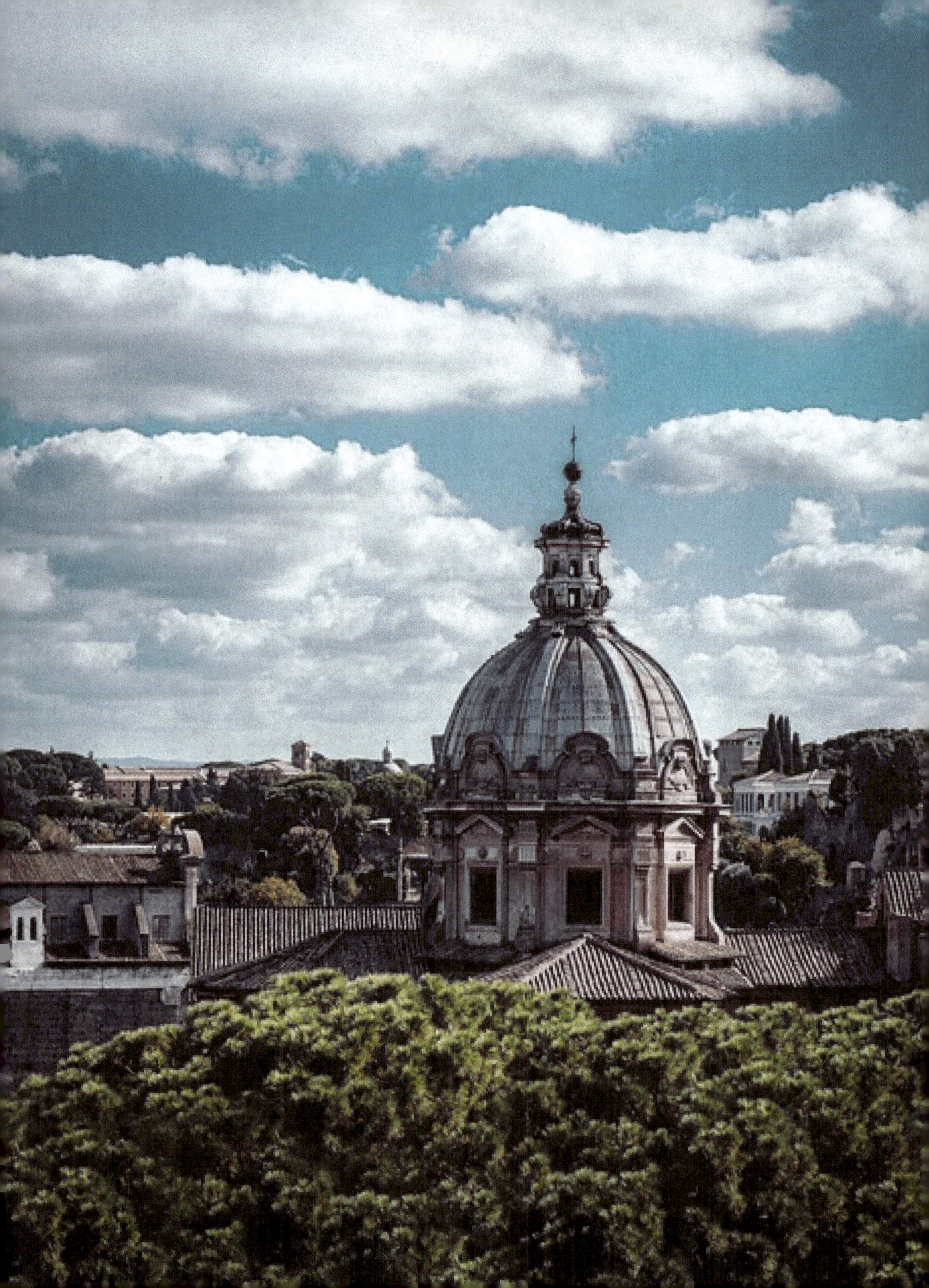

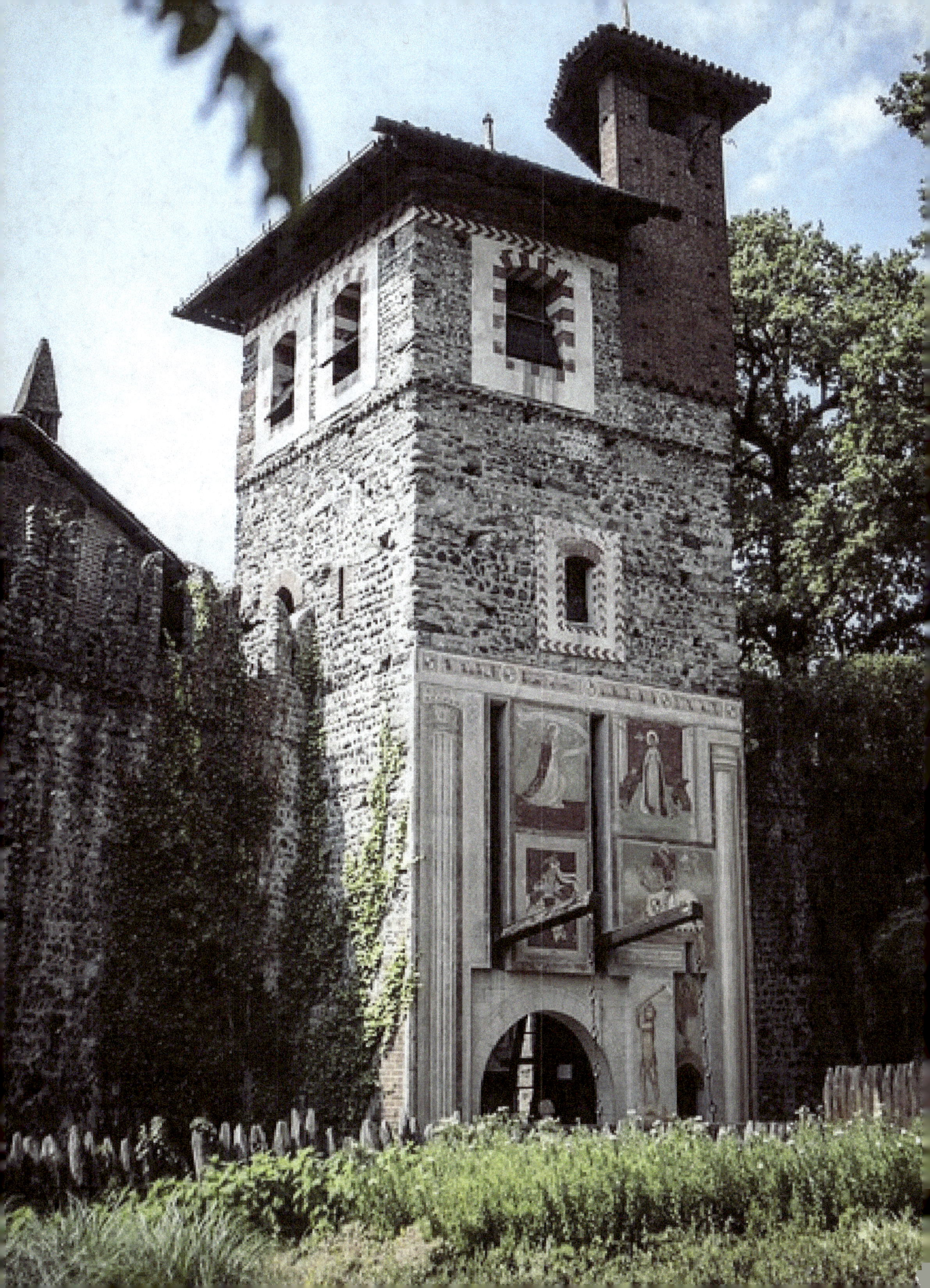

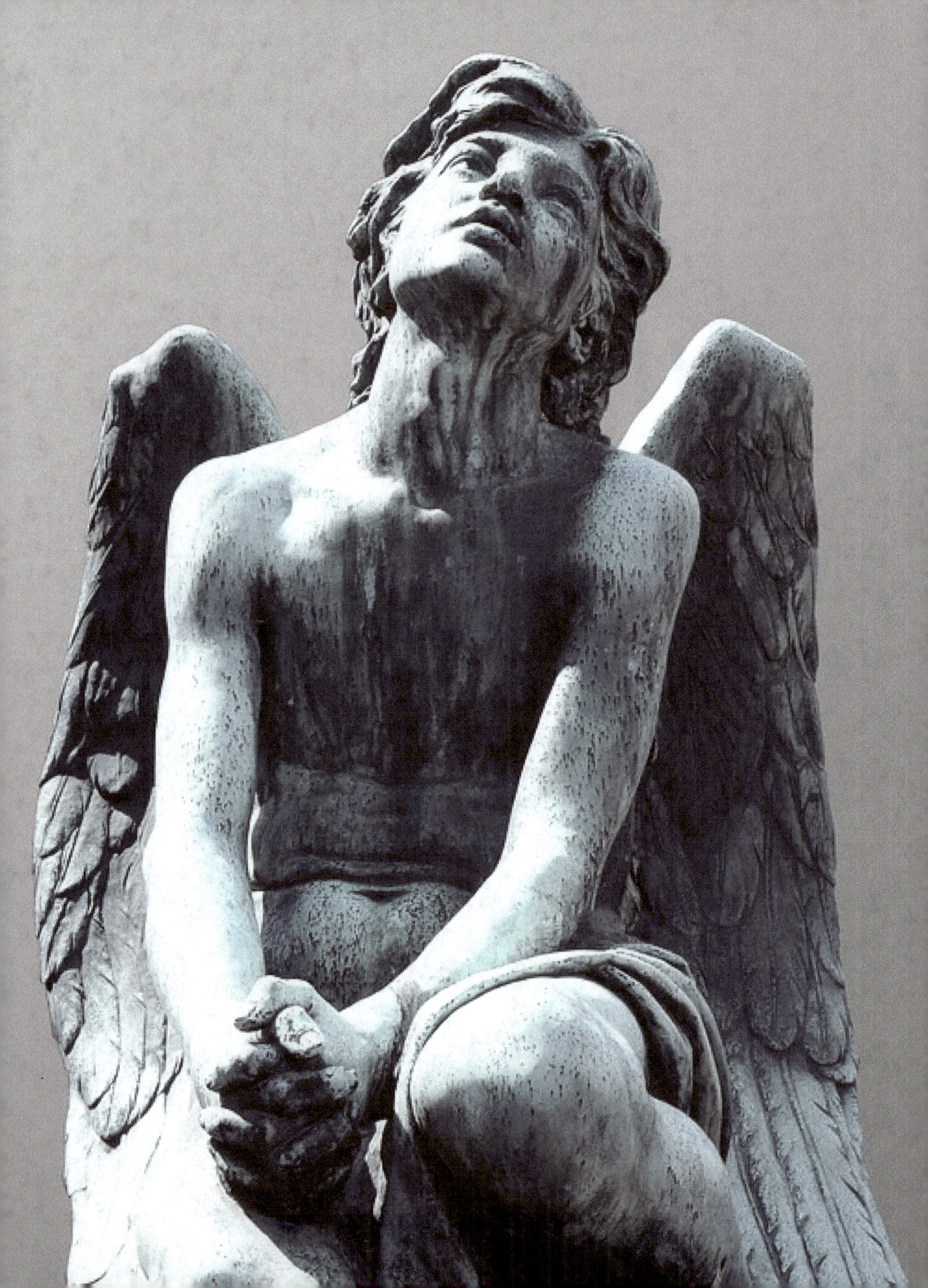

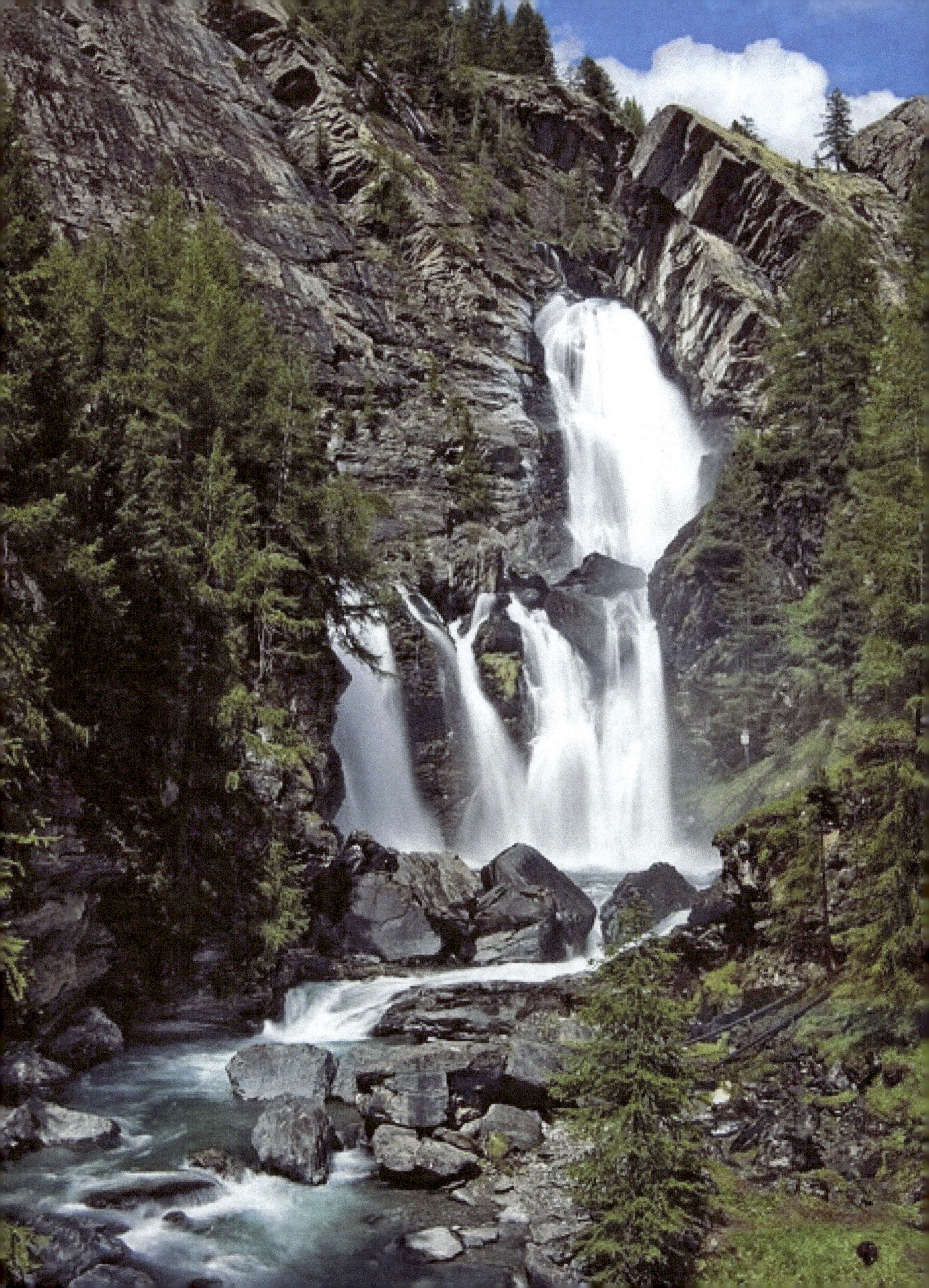

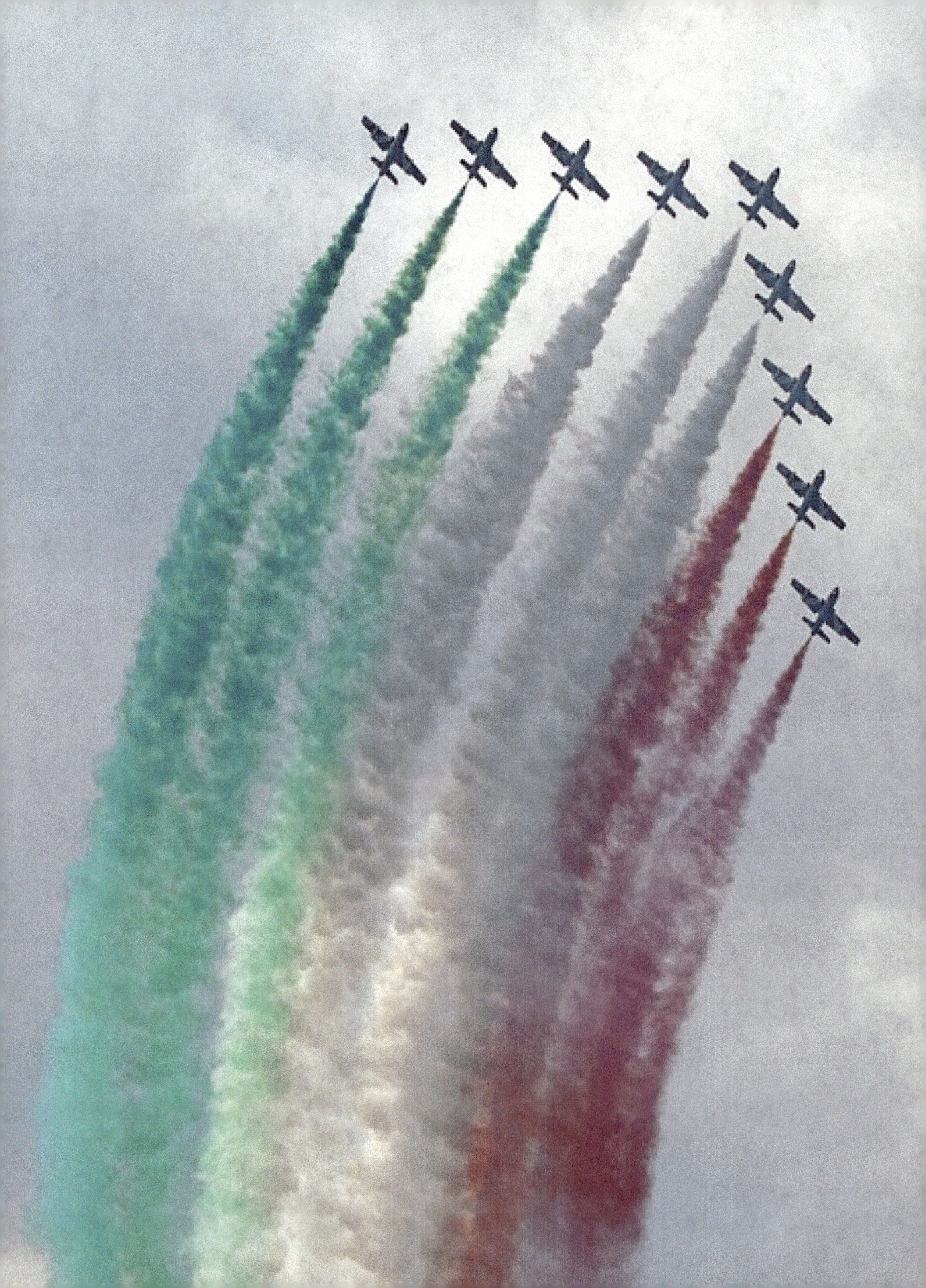

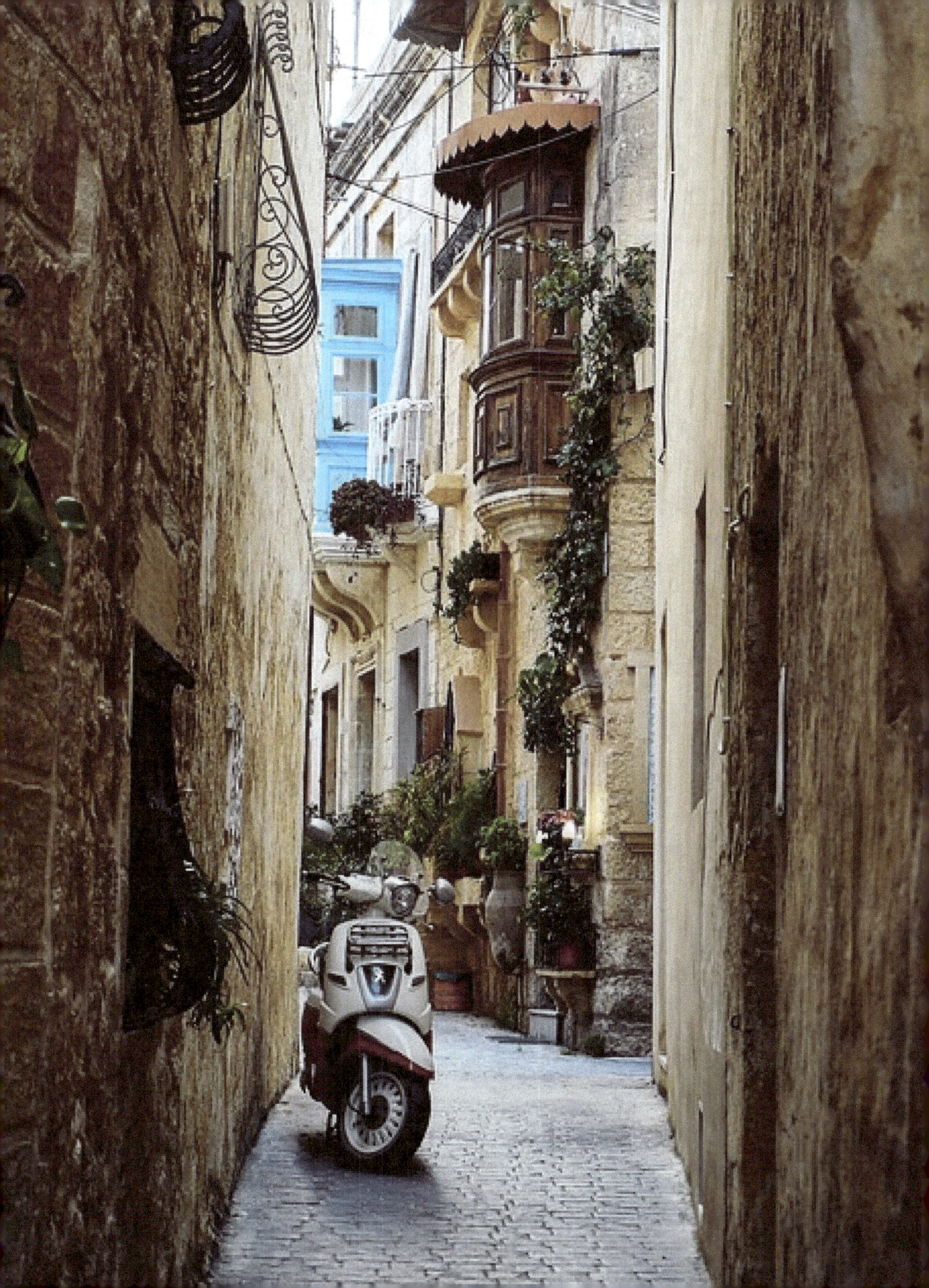

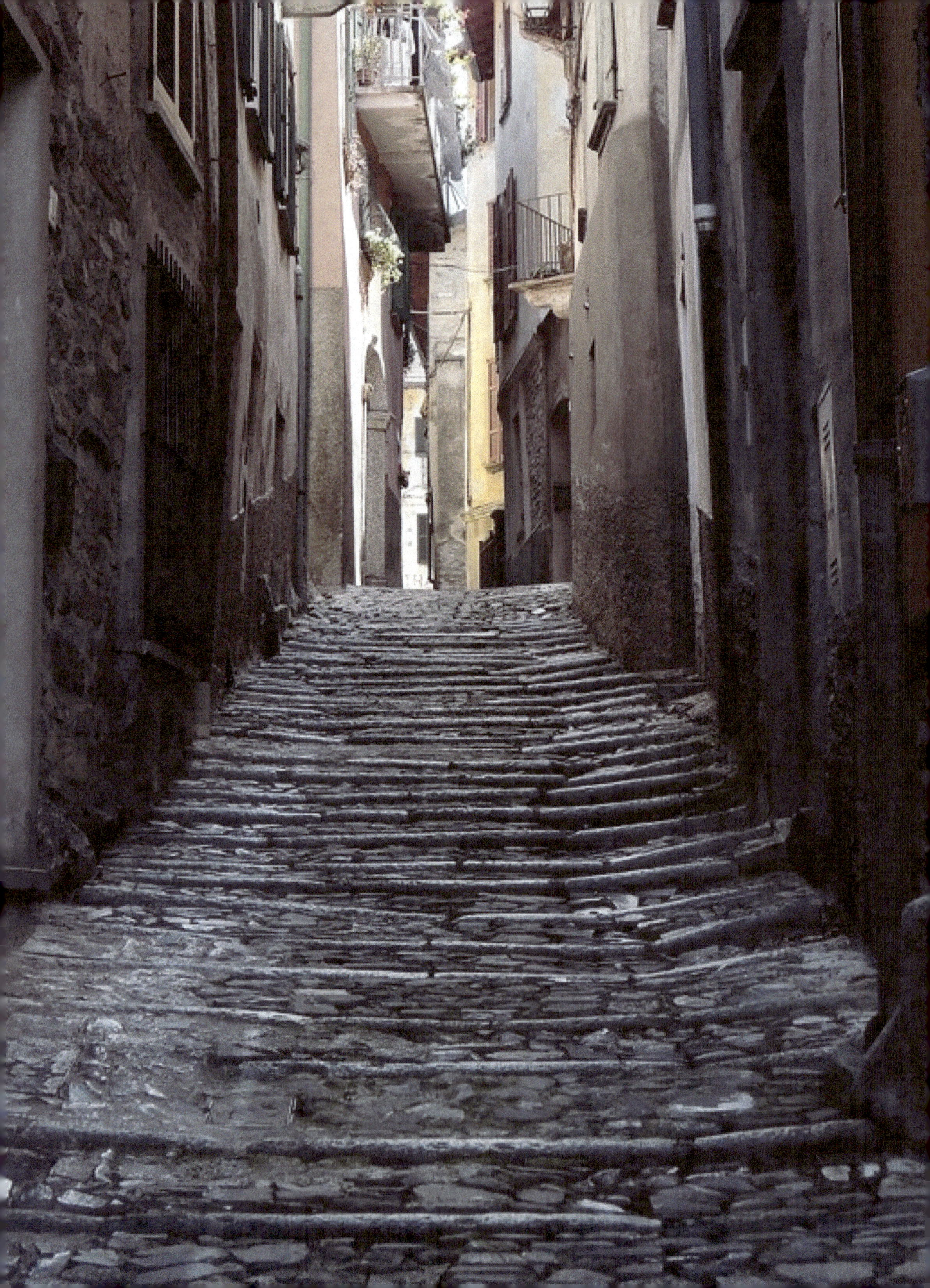

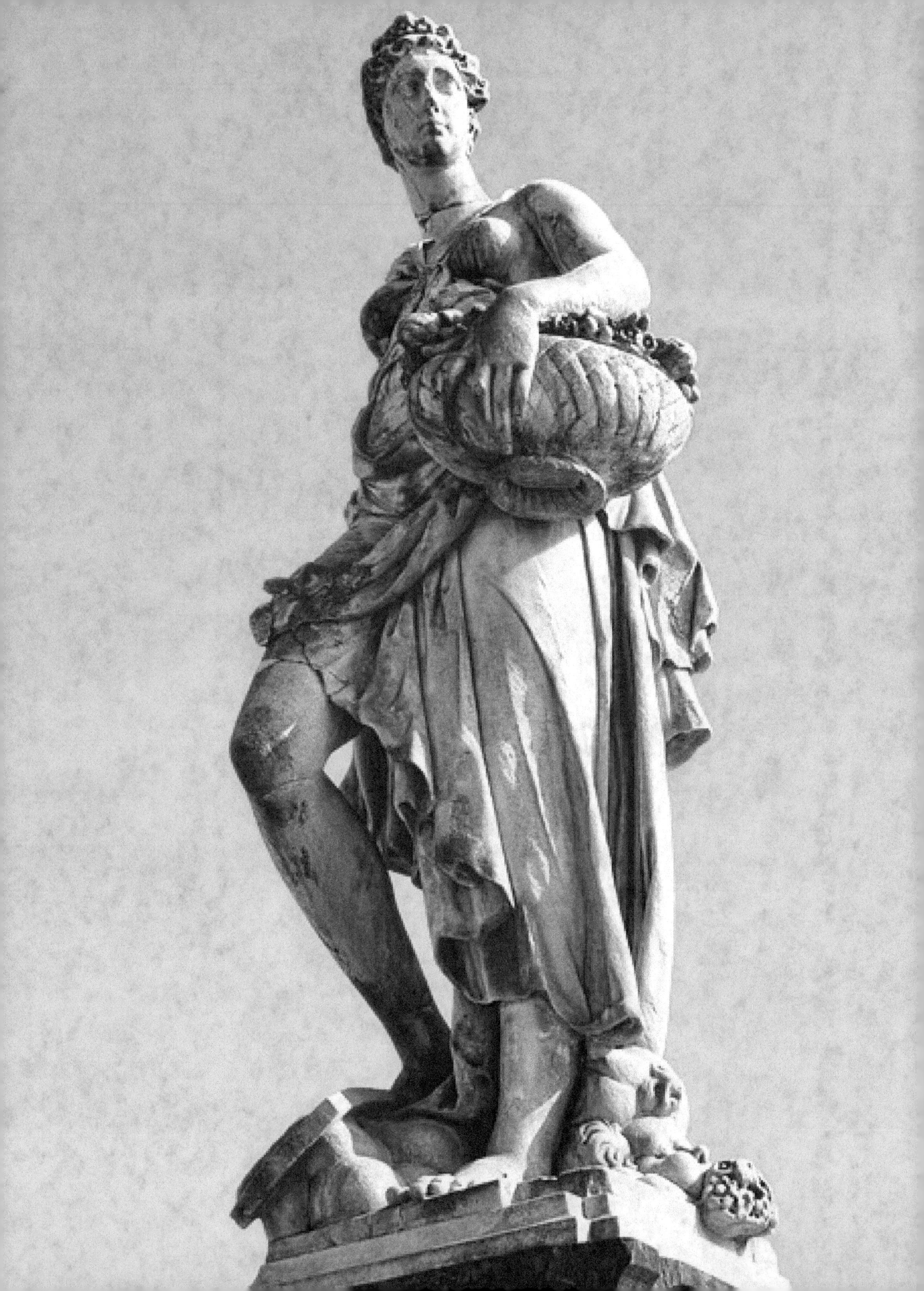

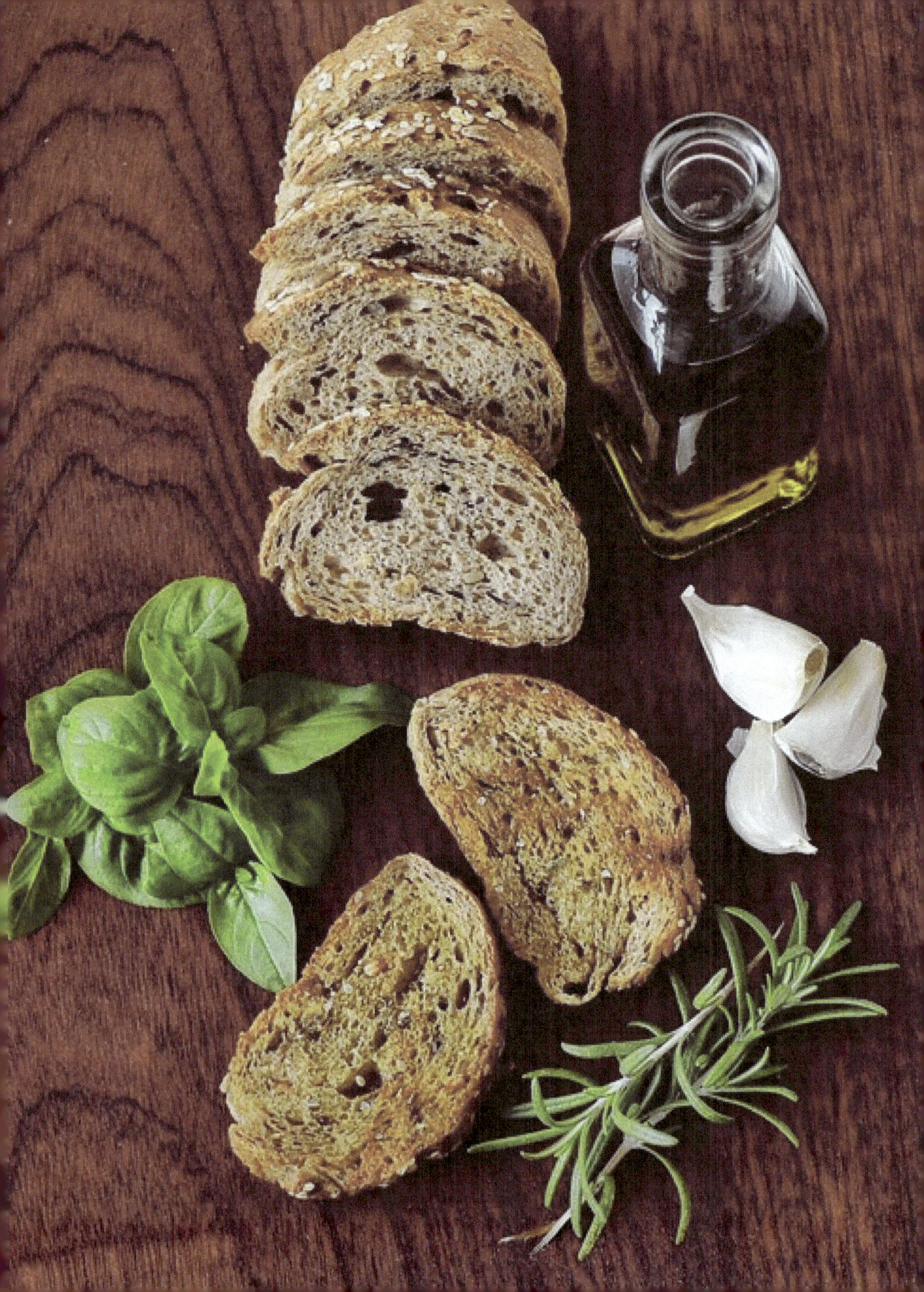

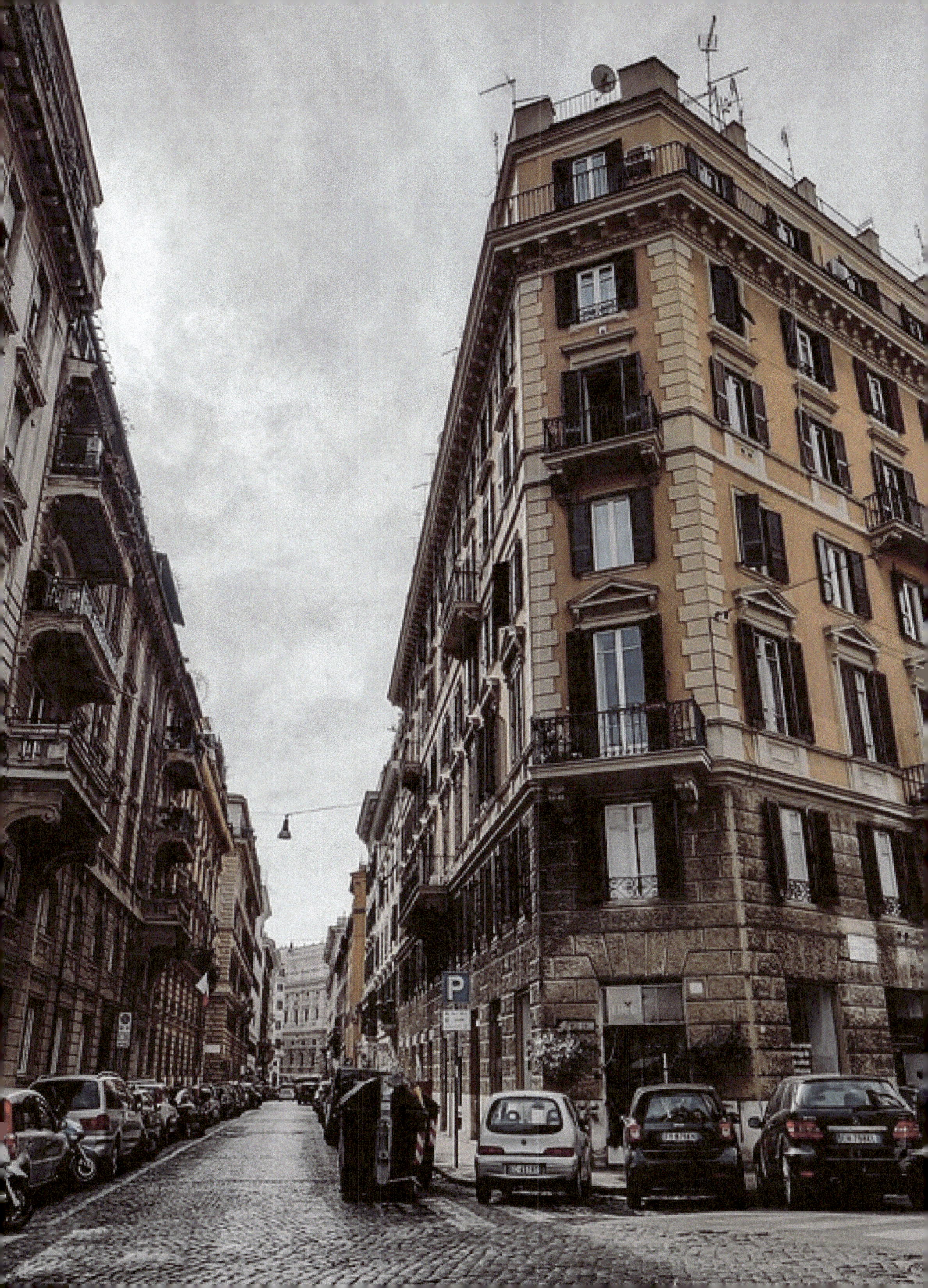
P

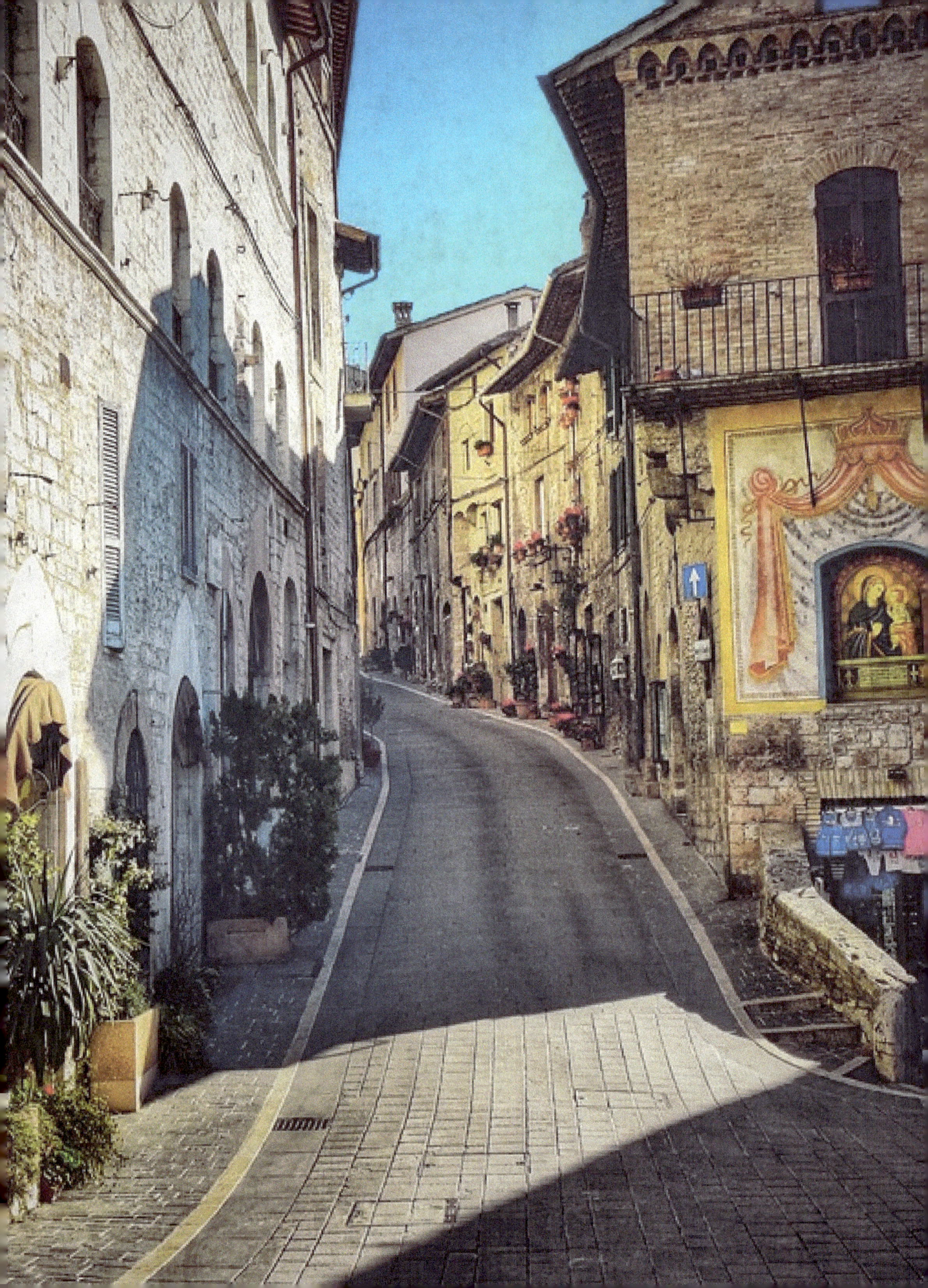

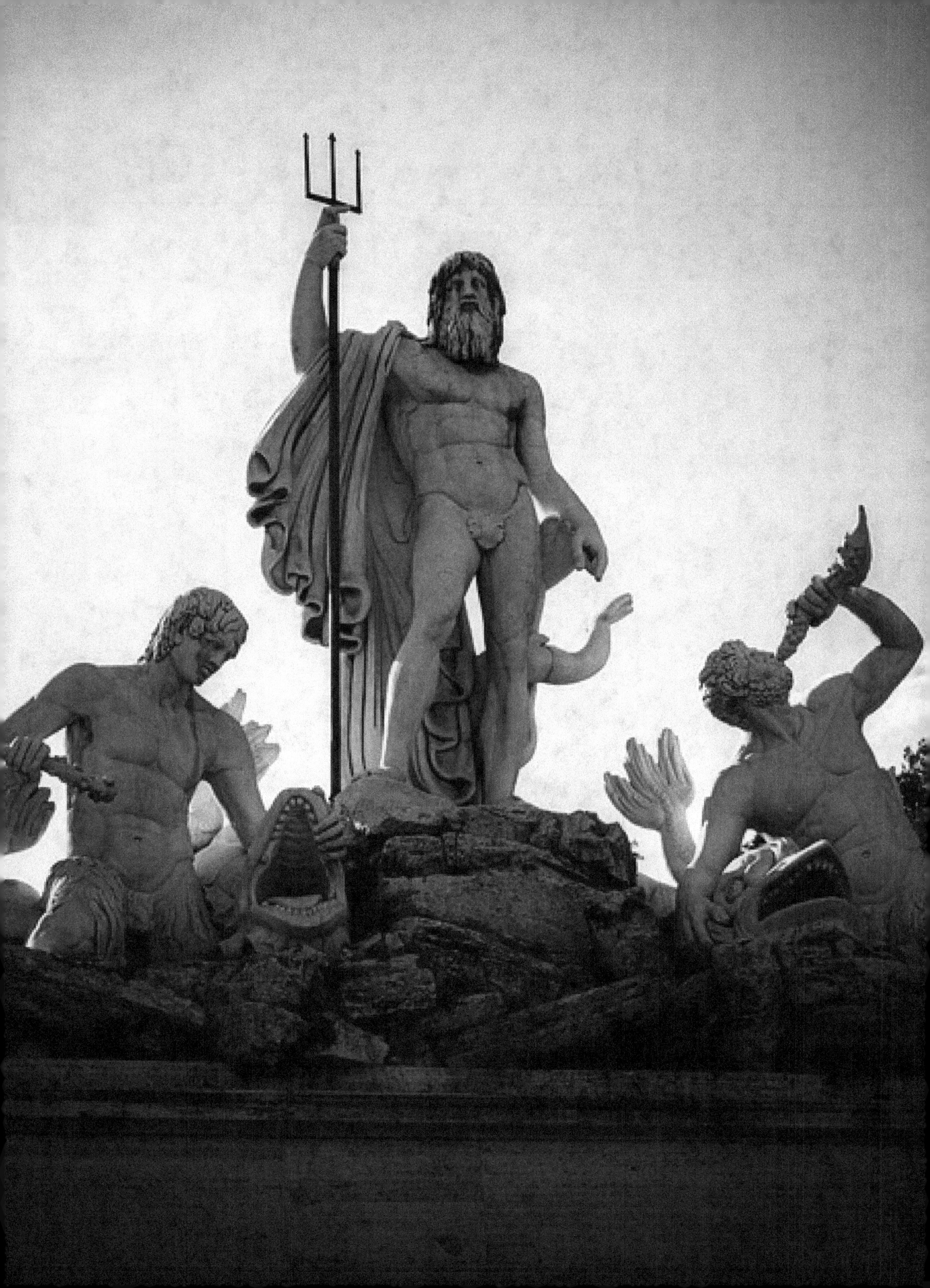

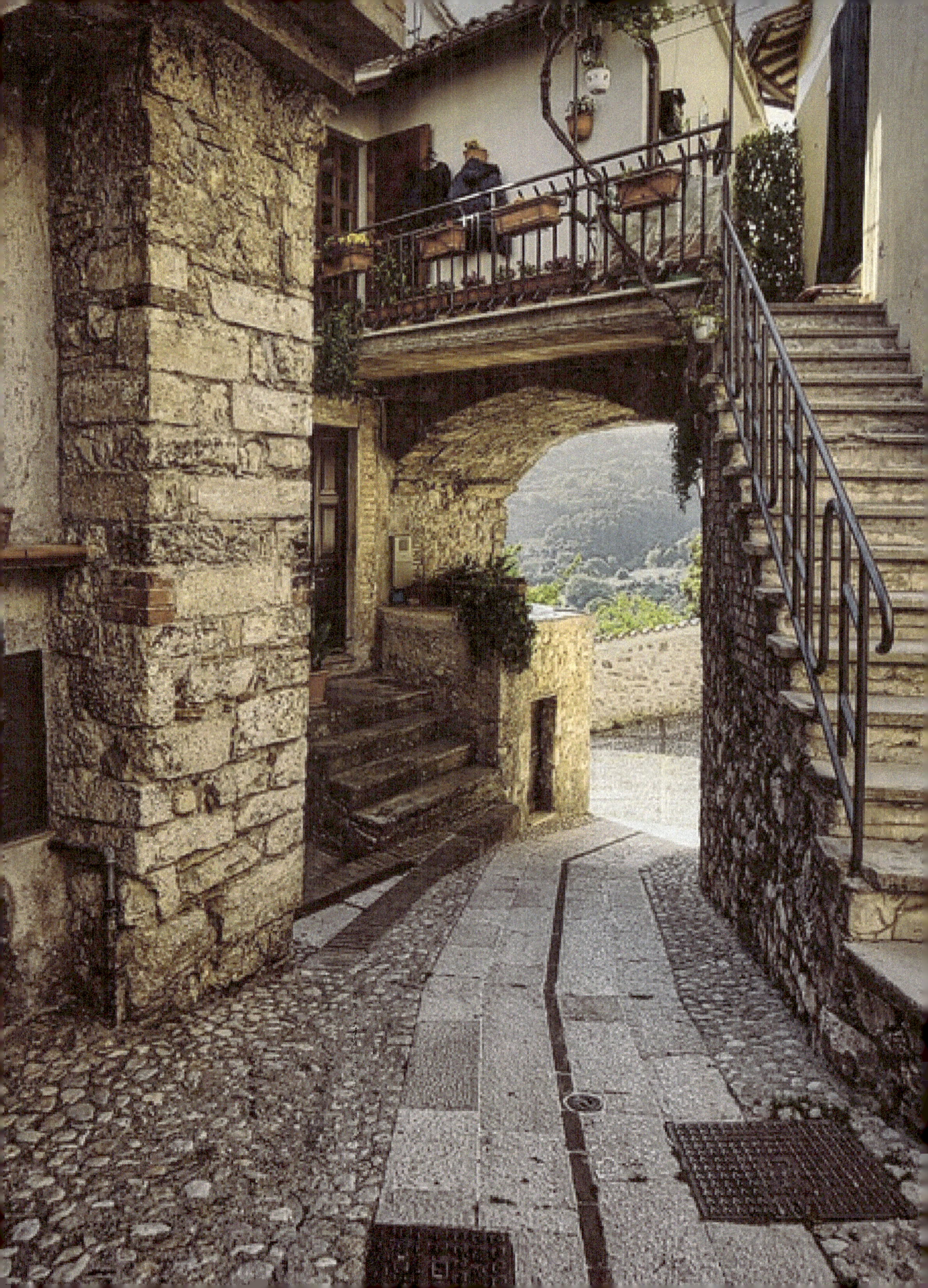

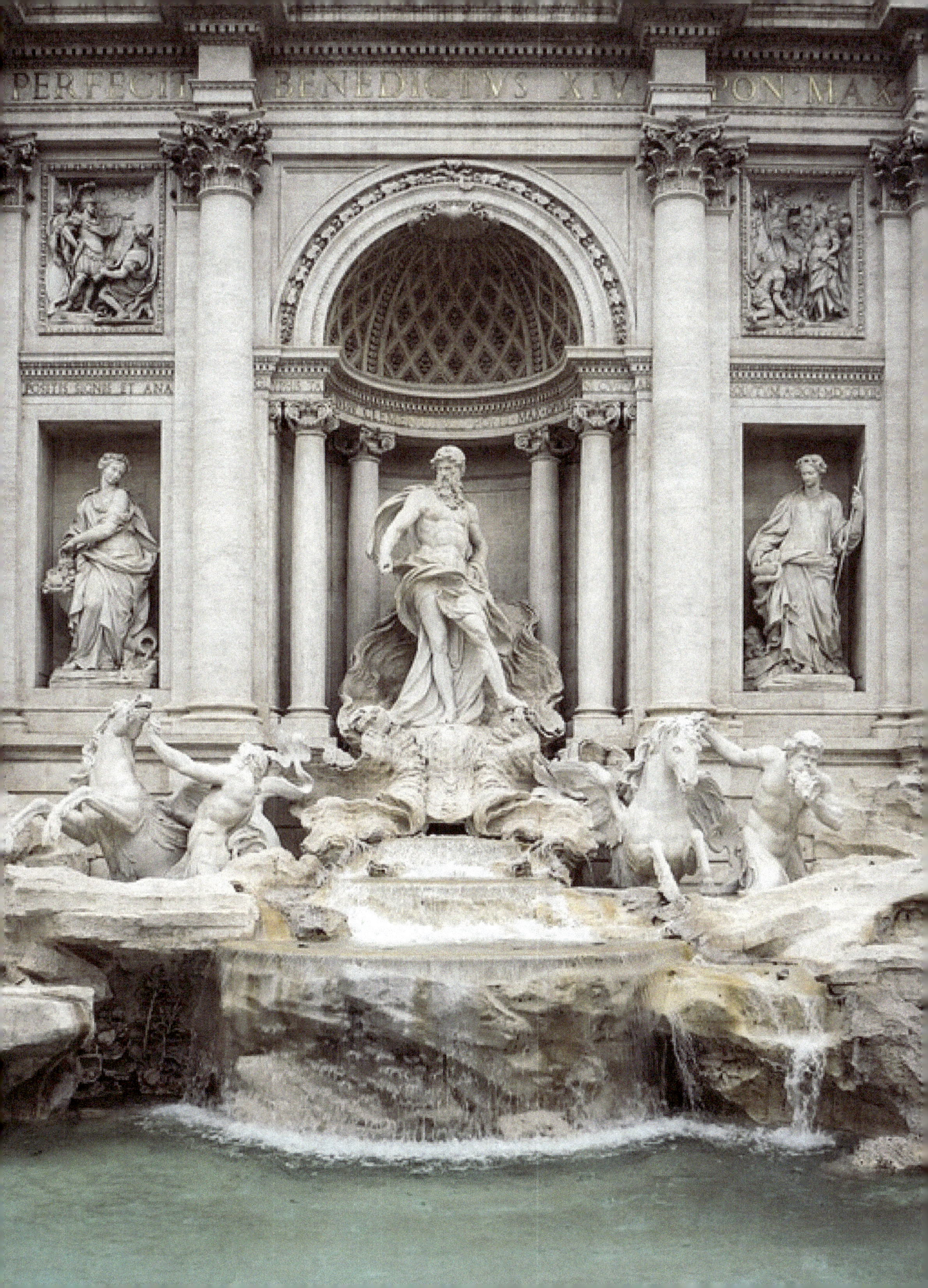
PERFECIT BENEDICTVS XIV PON·MAX

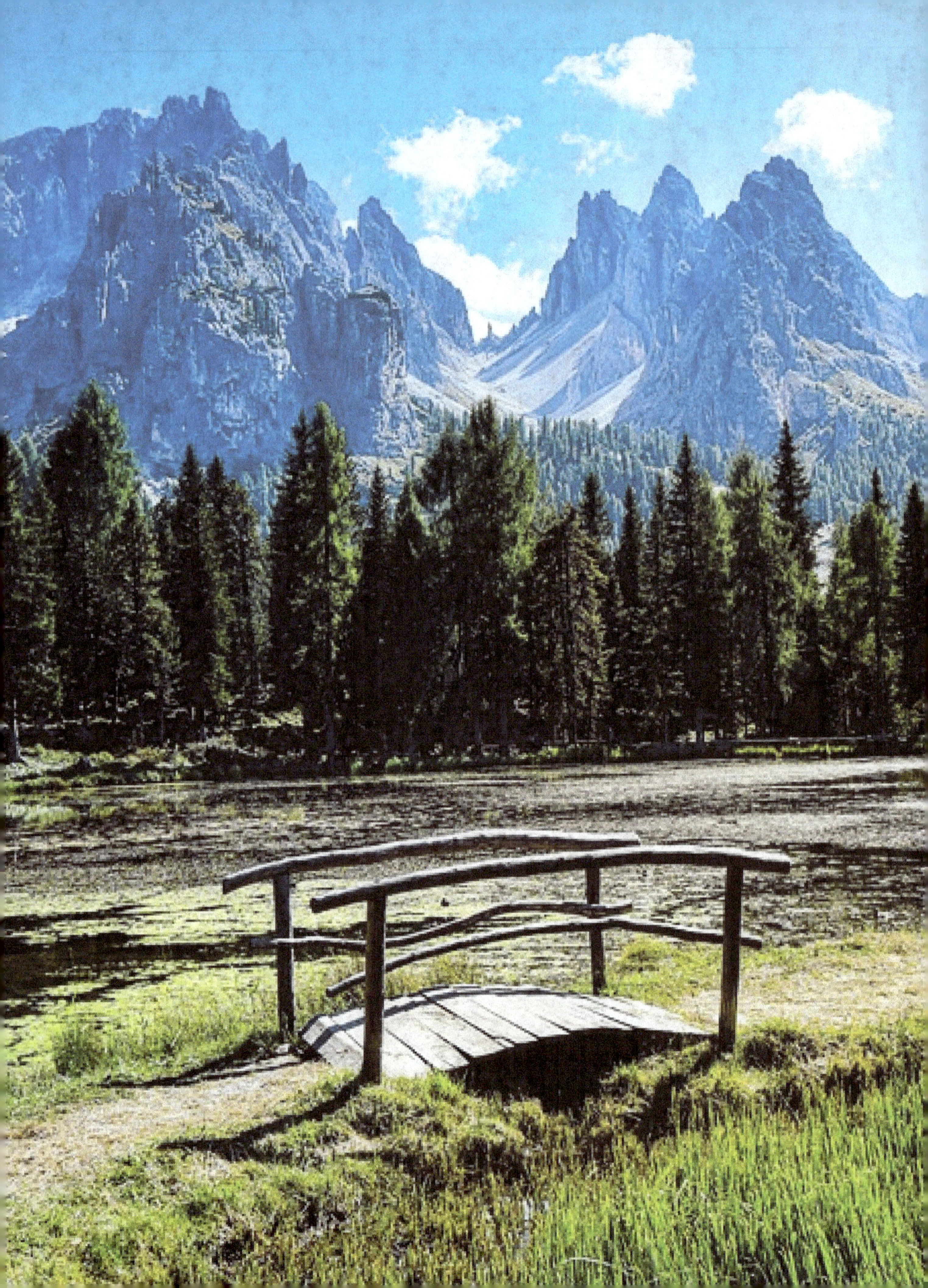

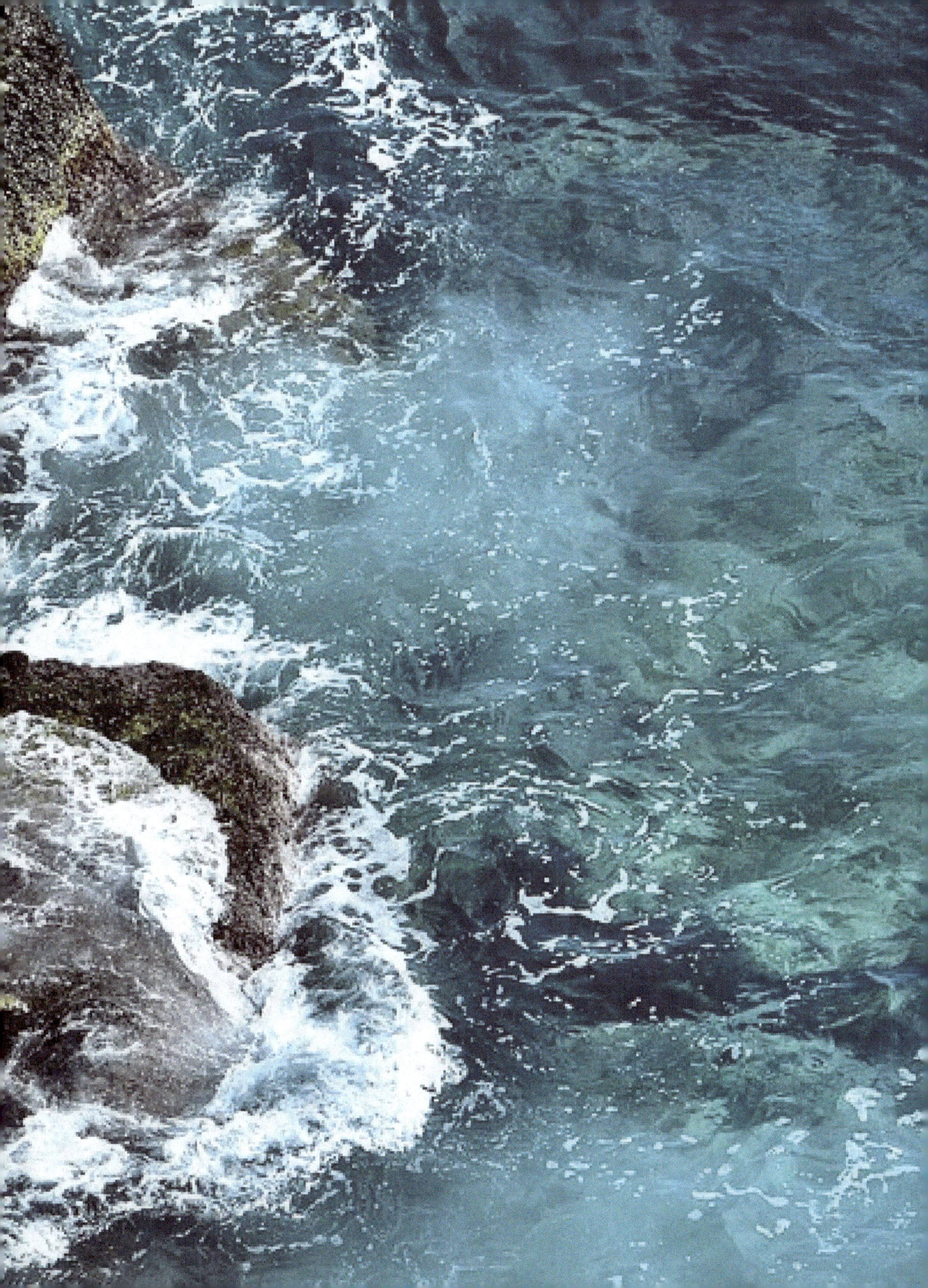

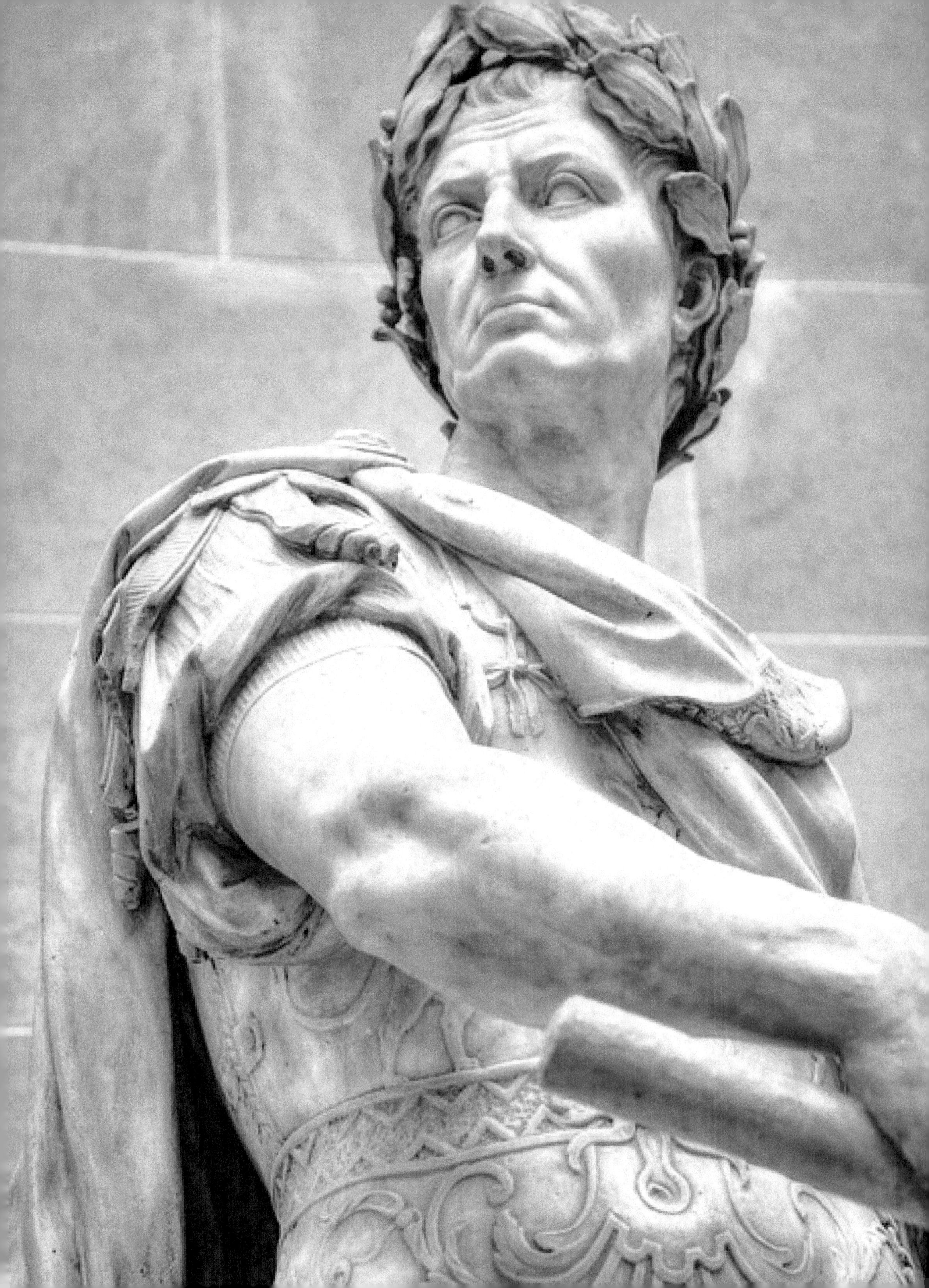

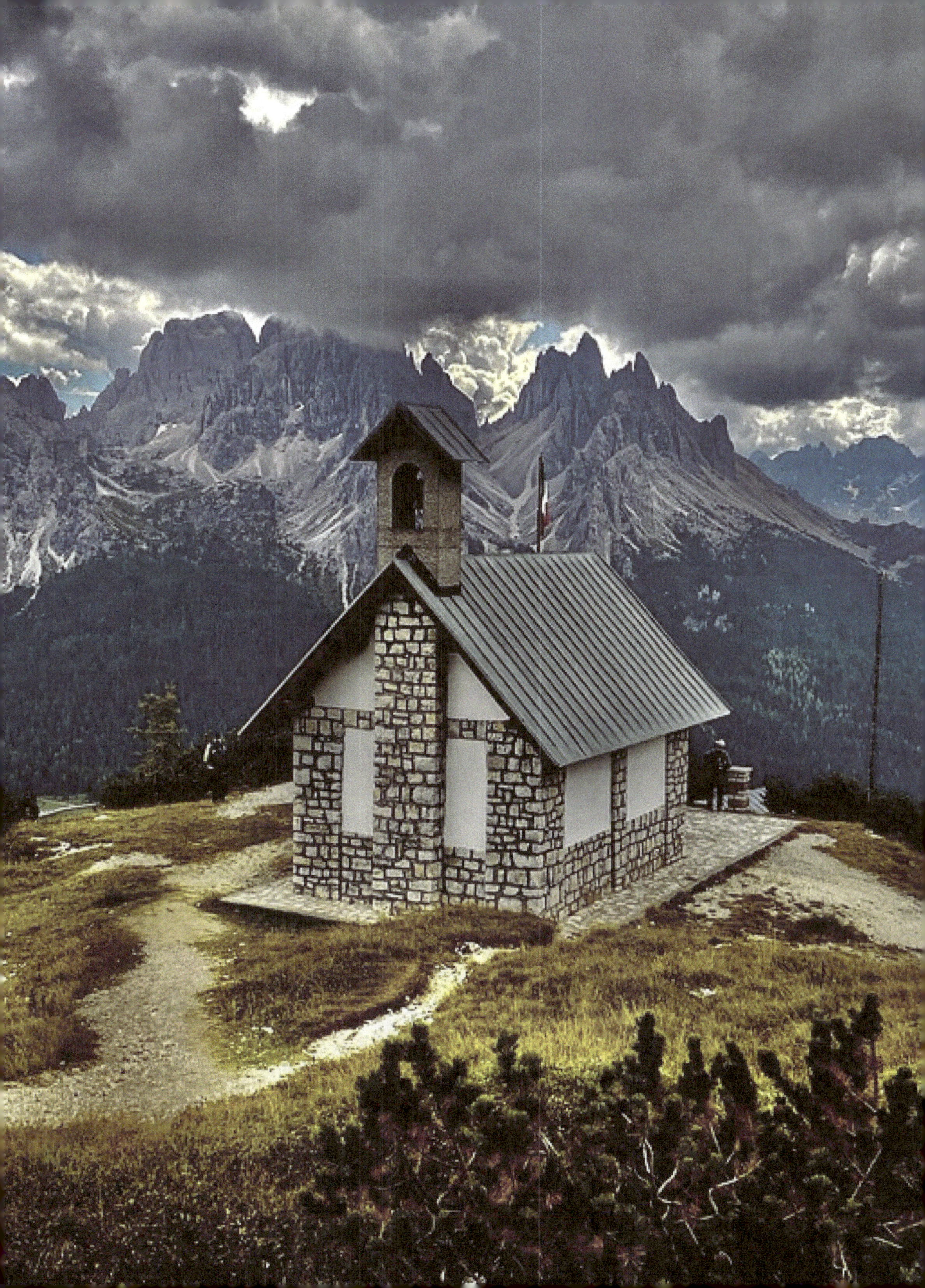

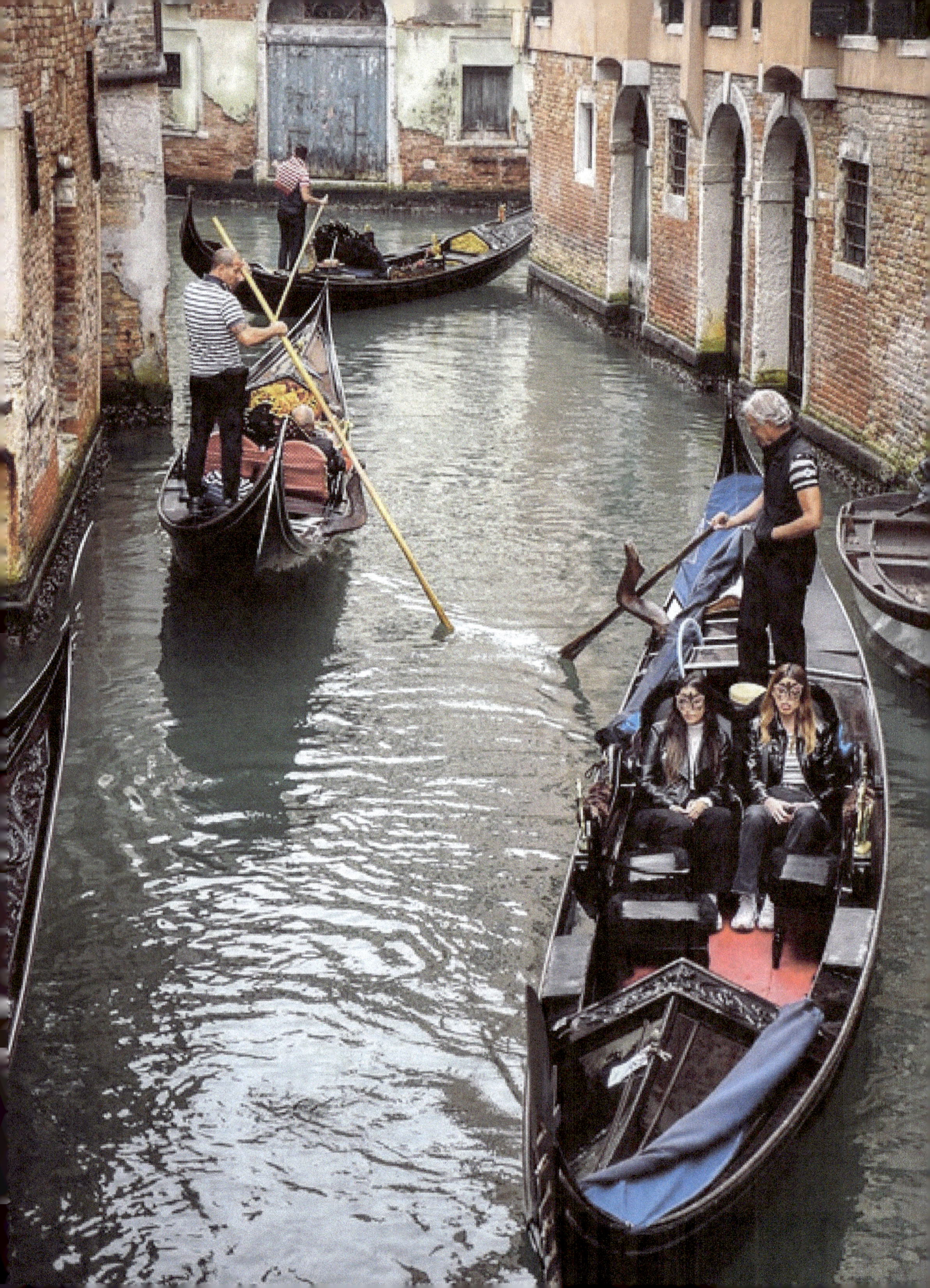

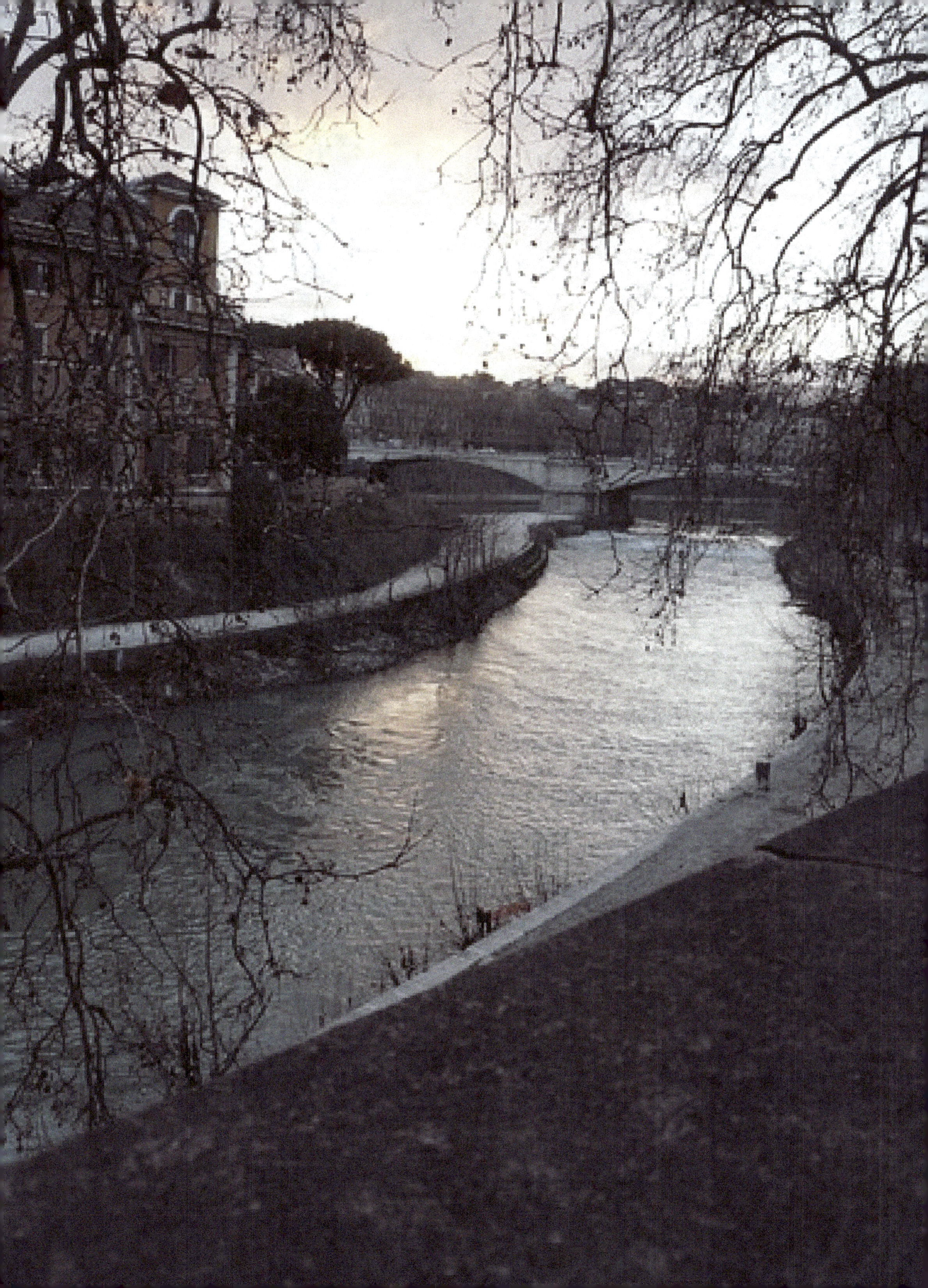

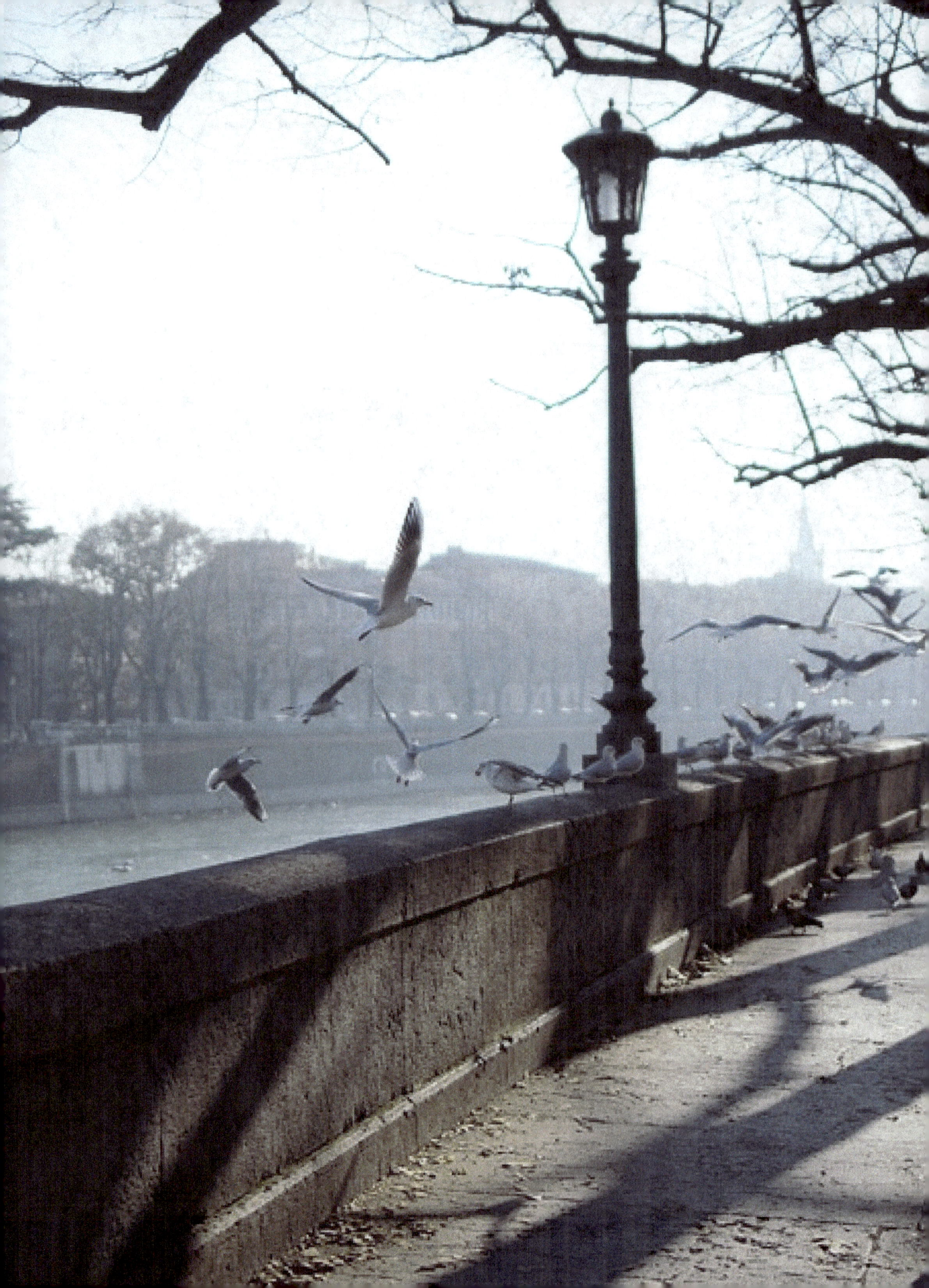

www.ingramcontent.com/pod-product-compliance
Lightning Source LLC
Chambersburg PA
CBHW080231220526
45467CB00037B/3044
9798388705808